Raising More
with Less

An Essential Fundraising Guide for Nonprofit Professionals and Board Members

Amy Eisenstein, CFRE

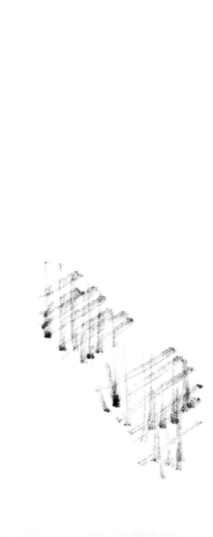

Raising More

with Less

An Essential Fundraising Guide for
Nonprofit Professionals and Board Members

Raising More with Less: An Essential Fundraising Guide for Nonprofit Professionals and Board Members

One of the In the Trenches™ series

Published by
CharityChannel Press, an imprint of CharityChannel LLC
30021 Tomas, Suite 300
Rancho Santa Margarita, CA 92688-2128 USA

charitychannel.com

ISBN: 978-1-938077-01-2

Library of Congress Control Number:

13 12 11 10 9 8 7 6 5 4 3 2 1

Printed in the United States of America

This and most CharityChannel Press books are available at special quantity discounts for bulk purchases for sales promotions, premiums, fundraising, or educational use. For information, contact CharityChannel Press, 30021 Tomas, Suite 300, Rancho Santa Margarita, CA 92688-2128 USA. +1 949-589-5938

About the Author

Amy Eisenstein, MPA, CFRE is also the author of *50 A$ks in 50 Weeks: A Guide to Better Fundraising for Your Small Development Shop* and is a contributing author to *You and Your Nonprofit: Practical Advice and Tips from the CharityChannel Professional Community.* Through writing, speaking, and consulting, Amy helps nonprofit staff and board members raise more money for the organizations they love.

Amy is the Principal and Owner of Tri Point Fundraising, a full-service consulting firm that supports organizations with capital and annual campaigns, individual giving and major gifts programs, and provides board and staff member training and support. She is also a frequent speaker at conferences, meetings, and retreats.

Amy received her master's degree in Public Administration and Nonprofit Management from the Wagner Graduate School at New York University and her bachelor's degree from Douglass College at Rutgers University. Amy currently serves as the president-elect for the Association of Fundraising Professionals' New Jersey Chapter. She has been a Certified Fundraising Executive (CFRE) since 2004, and became a certified Master Trainer in 2009.

Amy can be reached at http://www.tripointfundraising.com.

Acknowledgments

As with any book, this one would not have been possible without the love, support, and contributions of many people. I would like to begin by thanking my wonderful friend, colleague, editor, and publisher, Stephen C. Nill, CEO of CharityChannel Press, whom I have had the pleasure of getting to know over the last few years.

This book has been improved thanks to the contributions and technical support of Tony Martignetti, principal of Martignetti Planned Giving Advisors, and Brian Brolin, principal of Bri the Web Guy.

Many thanks also go to my proofreaders in the field, all of whom brought great insight about working "in the trenches" of a nonprofit organization. This book has stronger content, more thorough explanations, and fewer grammatical errors thanks to Brenda Hebert, Ray Brush, Diana Rumsey, Leslie Shernofsky, Mike Zimmerman, Matthew Alcide, Kourtney Carson, Andy Dubosky, Jo Ann Marianne, and David Eisenstein.

My gratitude also goes to you, and all of the other hardworking executive directors, board members, and development staff members who have entrusted me to help make certain they achieve their organization's missions, which would not be possible without additional resources. Thanks to your passion and commitment, the world is a better place.

And last but not least, to my loving husband and children, Alan, Ethan, and Zoe, who have been only mildly neglected throughout the writing process.

Contents

Chapter Nine

Chapter Ten

A Final Word From the Author

Foreword

Fundraising can often be an isolating and lonely profession, especially in small and one-person development shops. It doesn't have to be that way. Amy's book, *Raising More with Less: An Essential Fundraising Guide for Nonprofit Professionals and Board Members*, is the perfect companion to accompany you in your work in raising funds for your organization.

Raising More with Less is for beginners in the field of fundraising and the nonprofit sector, as well as seasoned nonprofit professionals who want to brush up and refresh their fundraising skills. It is part of the CharityChannel Press *In the Trenches* series, and, like the other books in the series, is written in a particularly fun, upbeat style—as if you're chatting with Amy at a local coffee shop.

In my role as the nonprofit expert at About.com, I regularly review books targeted for nonprofit audiences. In fact, I first became aware of Amy when I reviewed her first book, *50 Asks in 50 Weeks: A Guide to Better Fundraising for Your Small Development Shop*. As with her first book, I was immediately impressed with Amy's here's-how-to-do-it approach to fundraising. She has a special way of breaking down the potentially complex and often frightening topic of fundraising, so that it's easy to understand and implement. I've become one of her many fans.

Raising More with Less touches on many of the concepts about operating a successful small development shop introduced in *50 Asks,* but goes substantially beyond by providing new and significantly more information. To make things as useful as possible, she provides numerous worksheets, lists, and examples. If you follow the steps Amy has provided, it seems obvious that you will be able to raise significantly more money for your organization.

Joanne Fritz, Ph.D.
Guide to Nonprofit, Charitable Organizations
About.com

Introduction

Every nonprofit organization I've ever encountered wants to raise more money and, honestly, most need serious help with their approach to fundraising. If you are a board member or professional staff member working for a nonprofit and want to raise more money for your organization, you've come to the right place.

This book is for you if you:

◆ Are just starting a career in fundraising.

◆ Are an executive director or CEO of a nonprofit.

◆ Are responsible for a new organization that has limited or no history or experience with fundraising.

◆ Are a board member who has been charged with the responsibility of leading fundraising efforts.

◆ Are a seasoned fundraising professional and want to brush up on the basics and get some new ideas.

◆ Have become stale and want to get reenergized and reinvigorated about fundraising.

The terms "fundraising" and "development" will be used interchangeably throughout this book, as they are used in the world of philanthropy. In the field of fundraising, "development" is often the term of choice instead of fundraising. For example, you may be familiar with the term "development director" as the person in charge of fundraising.

Let's pretend you've just been hired at a nonprofit to run the development office. (Okay, okay, so maybe you've been there for a few years. That's not important.) What is the first thing you should do to get your new development office off the ground (or improve the one you have)?

If you're in a small development office, you have an amazing opportunity before you. Whether you are the executive director, a development director, or a fundraising volunteer, you have the chance to shape your development program and make a significant difference in the lives of others. Whether or not you raise enough money to help fulfill your mission is in large part up to you. I've had the exciting challenge of creating two development shops from scratch during my career, in addition to working with dozens of clients at small and large organizations, which has been both rewarding and challenging. Throughout this book, I'm going to share my successes and failures with you, so you can learn from my experience.

This book will take you step-by-step through creating or improving your development program, whether your organization has no paid fundraising staff members or is fortunate enough to have one full-time staffer or more. My definition of a small development shop is when a few people (staff and/or volunteers) are doing it all. In a small development office, you are responsible for more than one aspect of development (you don't have the luxury of having a dedicated person for special events, another for writing grants, someone for individual solicitations, a database management specialist, and so on). In other words, you do it all! Your day should not be boring as you bounce from event planner to grant writer to database manager extraordinaire.

This book is meant to serve as a resource and guide for you, if you want to accomplish your organization's mission. Think that's a tall order? It is. How are you going to achieve your mission if you don't have the funds to do so?

If that sounds like you and your organization, you've come to the right place! I promise that if you follow the steps in this book and put the tools and techniques to use, you will raise more money for your organization this year without any additional resources or staff members.

You will, however, need to work smarter, follow some proven strategies and methods, and follow a plan (that you will create). As you know, fundraising isn't always easy, but it can be fun and rewarding.

Chapter Summaries

Chapter One: Eight Simple Steps to Creating an Outstanding Development Office (or Improving Your Existing One). Chapter One sets the stage for the entire book and outlines the necessary steps to start a new development office or supercharge your existing fundraising program. Read this chapter to gain an understanding of what to do next, no matter where you are.

Chapter Two: Fundraising Basics: More Than Odds and Ends. Chapter Two reviews some of the basics of fundraising, which is a necessary foundation on which to build subsequent chapters. It is a review and outline of tried-and-true fundraising techniques and tools.

Chapter Three: Building the Fundraising Board of Your Dreams. Chapter Three covers the basics of boards with regards to fundraising. In Chapter Three, you will learn why it is critical to have a strong fundraising board in order to have a solid overall fundraising program.

Chapter Four: Creating a Fundraising Plan for Success. Chapter Four talks about the importance of having a fundraising plan, creating a baseline and developing goals, writing your plan, and following it. This chapter provides a basic plan outline for you to use and move forward.

Chapter Five: Technology, E-Philanthropy, and Social Media. Chapter Five covers the use of technology to enhance your fundraising efforts. This chapter explains the importance of developing an online fundraising and social media presence, and how to do so.

Chapter Six: Building Your Annual Fund through Bulk Mail. Chapter Six focuses on how to use bulk mail (snail mail and electronic) to grow your annual fund and base of supporters. You will learn what an annual fund is, and why it is important to your organization.

Chapter Seven: Face-to-Face Fundraising: Facing Your Fear. Chapter Seven might be the most important chapter in the book. This chapter shows you how to start and succeed with individual, face-to-face fundraising, something that many nonprofits avoid like the plague. Learn how to identify, cultivate, solicit, and steward your best prospective donors.

Chapter Eight: Simple Planned Gifts that Anyone Can Manage. Chapter Eight teaches you the importance of incorporating a planned giving program, primarily bequests, into your development program and plan. Bequests are easy to solicit and accept, and are often the largest individual gifts your organization ever receives.

Chapter Nine: Event Fundraising and Corporate Sponsorship. Chapter Nine reviews the *why* and *how-to* of event fundraising. It will ensure that you make the most of your special events through sponsorship and post-event, donor follow-up.

Chapter Ten: Grant Writing and Foundation Funding. Chapter Ten focuses on grant writing from start to finish. There is a special focus on building relationships with funders, which is the key to successful grant funding.

Final Thoughts and Next Steps

I've saved some of the best for last, so don't skip this part. It talks about how to raise more money by keeping your current donors.

How to Use this Book

Throughout this book you will find sidebars, tables, and checklists to help you create an efficient and effective development office as well as jump-start your fundraising efforts.

Below are the types of sidebars you will find throughout the book:

◆ Definitions

◆ Stories from the Real World

◆ To-Do Lists

◆ Practical Tips

◆ 50 Asks in 50 Weeks

Why Fundraising?

Before you turn the page, I want you to sit back, close your eyes (after you finish reading, of course) and imagine all the things you and your organization could accomplish with more financial resources. Would you cure a disease? Feed more children? Improve education? Clean the environment?

Now think about that same world without your work and your organization. That sad world will be the reality if you don't raise the funds necessary to accomplish your goals and dreams.

With that in mind, let's get started. I know you can do it!

If you need any additional support or help, I'm here for you.

◆ Read my blog posts and engage in conversation with me and other experts on the CharityChannel site at charitychannel. com.

◆ Reach me at amy@tripointfundraising.com.

◆ Follow me on Twitter @amyeisenstein.

◆ Like me on Facebook at http://www.facebook.com/ TriPointFundraising.

Best wishes for your fundraising success!

Chapter One

Eight Simple Steps to Creating an Outstanding Development Office (or Improving Your Existing One)

IN THIS CHAPTER

---→ Learn how to start a development office from scratch at a new organization.

---→ Identify the first steps to take when starting a new fundraising role at an established organization.

---→ Improve the existing development program for which you are responsible.

Whether it's your first day on the job at a new organization, or you've been at your organization for many years, you're reading this because you want guidance on how to get your development shop off on the right footing or significantly improve an existing one. If you fall into the latter category, do not despair! It's never too late to learn new skills, improve processes, or raise more money for your organization.

Some of the issues covered in this chapter will also be covered in more detail later in the book. Even so, I recommend that you read this chapter to make certain that you have a solid foundation and to learn the eight most important steps to creating or refining your development program. If you only do these eight steps and nothing else, you will be well on your way to creating a successful fundraising program.

Step 1: Recruiting a Board, and Getting to Know Your Board Members

A well-built and active board is one of the most essential components of operating an effective development program.

Do you have board members who are engaged in fundraising? Do they identify new, prospective donors, help with solicitation, and assist by saying thank you to donors?

A **Fundraising Board** (as opposed to a non-fundraising board) is a board that has a "culture of giving" and board members who help with all aspects of fundraising. Every board should be a fundraising board.

finition

Unfortunately, many organizations do not recruit board members who are expected to help with fundraising, and therefore, board members do not participate as they should. When this occurs, we say a board has no "culture" of fundraising.

I believe it takes an average of about three years to turn a non-fundraising board into a fundraising board. If you're just getting started, it may take less time than that, because you are either creating a board from scratch, or you've been hired because the board is ready for a change. Either way, it's time to have a fundraising board so you can jump-start your fundraising!

If you are new to an existing organization, the first thing to do is meet your current board members, starting with the board chair or president. Plan to meet with each one individually during your first month on the job. This is a major priority. The goal of each meeting is to determine the following:

◆ How board members got involved with the organization.

◆ How long they have been involved and any positions they've held at the organization.

◆ Why they stay involved.

◆ Their overall thoughts on the organization.

◆ Their opinion of the reputation of the organization in the community.

◆ Their thoughts on how the board operates and is managed.

◆ Ideas for improvements.

◆ Thoughts on fundraising and board giving.

◆ Other thoughts they'd like to share.

If you've been at an organization for many years, but don't know the answers to some of these key questions, you should take the time to meet with each board member individually as well. This will help you get to know each board member in a more personal way, and start moving your organization in the direction of creating a fundraising board.

If you have the opportunity to recruit new board members right away, you will want to create a board member job description and a board expectation form. (See Chapter Three for examples and additional details.)

One way of ensuring a strong fundraising board is to recruit board members who have the expectation that they will make a contribution to your organization and help raise funds. You should also have appropriate development targets to aim for, for the board as a whole, and tasks for board members themselves to complete.

Step 2: Identify and Meet Your Largest and Most Loyal Donors

After you've met with your board members, the next step in creating a successful development program is identifying your largest and most loyal donors. I will get into detail about this in Chapter Seven on face-to-face giving, but for now it's important to make sure you know who your organization's best donors are.

Hopefully, you will be able to quickly identify your best (biggest and most loyal) donors from your database. This involves running lists of your largest and most loyal donors. Once you've done so, make a list of your top twenty best prospective donors and hang it on the wall above your desk. This week, call each one to introduce yourself and schedule a time to meet. (More details can be found in Chapter Seven.)

My suggestions for a phone or in-person meeting with your best donors include:

◆ Thank them for their past giving (it doesn't matter that the gifts were made in the past or that you weren't there to witness them). Donors can never be thanked enough.

◆ Find out why they are interested in your cause and in your organization.

◆ Ask why they started giving and what makes them continue to give.

◆ Ask how the organization could improve and what they love most about your organization.

◆ Ask how they might like to become involved. Provide some examples of volunteer opportunities, including direct service, office work, committee service, etc.

◆ Provide an update about the program or service and let them know how their most recent donation was used.

> Your **Largest Donors** are those individuals who gave the most during the period being measured (during the last twelve months, for example). Be sure to identify donors who gave large, one-time amounts as well as smaller amounts multiple times during the year.
>
> **Loyal Donors** are those donors who have given multiple times over a period of years. For example, anyone who has given more than five times during the last seven years—at any level. This distinguishes loyal donors from large donors, because you would include your $25 annual donors on this list assuming that they have made multiple gifts at this level over several years.
>
> **(de)finition**

Note that I leave talking about the program until last. Novice fundraisers often make the mistake of believing that they need to tell prospective donors everything there is to know about the organization. By doing this, they neglect to take the time to get to know the individual they are speaking with. The conversation becomes one-sided and the donor tunes out. This is one of the worst possible outcomes from a donor meeting, because you are trying to engage the donors. By talking at them instead of engaging them with good questions, you end up alienating them.

You may know the expression, "ask for money and you'll get advice; ask for advice and you'll get money." People want to be engaged, have their thoughts heard and their opinions valued. If you take the time to ask their opinion, then your supporters will feel valued. Their inclination to support you will dramatically increase once they are involved and engaged.

Additional details on meeting your best donors are available in Chapter Seven, but the basic rule is to build relationships with them. If you're just starting out and you don't have any donors yet, don't worry. You will no doubt attract donors soon, and have the opportunity to build lasting relationships with each one.

Step 3: Review Your Website and Make an On-line Donation

If you're starting a new job, I hope you visited the organization's website before going on the first interview and certainly before accepting the job. That's what a vast majority of donors will do before deciding whether or not to make a donation.

If you've been at your organization for a while, when was the last time you visited your website? Is it updated regularly? Your website is the first thing prospective donors will use to judge your organization, so it has got to be good.

When you visit your website be sure to answer the following questions:

- ◆ Does it clearly and succinctly state your mission?
- ◆ Will a visitor easily and quickly understand what your organization does?
- ◆ Can visitors contact staff from your site by clicking a link in a staff directory?
- ◆ Can they find your address and phone number?
- ◆ Is it easy or complicated to donate to your organization online?
- ◆ Is a "donate now" button prominently displayed on the home page and every other page of your site?

Have you ever made a donation through your website? If not, how do you know what the donor experiences? Make a donation to your organization through your website today. That's right, put down the book and go make an online donation to your organization. Right now!

For more details on electronic fundraising, see Chapter Five, Technology, E-Philanthropy, and Social Media.

Step 4: Create Calendars with Deadlines

Analyze and Create a Calendar of Events and Mailings.

Is there an organized, comprehensive calendar of events at your organization? If you are new at the organization, this is one of the first tools you need to create or familiarize yourself with so you don't miss any deadlines or delay any projects or events.

A comprehensive fundraising calendar will include major events, mailing deadlines, grant deadlines, newsletters, email blasts and solicitations, and more.

Review the calendar from the perspective of your donors. How many mailings per year or per month will they receive? Your goal is to stay in front of them with interesting, relevant content and information, but not to overwhelm them. On average, try to send one mailing per month. It could be a newsletter, event invitation, or solicitation. Mailings can be sent electronically or traditionally (snail mail), although you will want to use a combination of traditional and electronic mail throughout the year and not rely too heavily on one or the other.

Create a Grants Calendar and Research New Opportunities.

This calendar is different from the general fundraising calendar above, as it is just for grant application and report deadlines. Identify all current grant deadlines, both report and reapplication deadlines, and make sure to meet deadlines and continue building relationships with current funders.

Depending on the number of grants your organization currently applies for and receives, you might want to consider doing some research to identify new potential sources of income.

For more information on grant research and building relationships with foundation funders, see Chapter Ten.

Step 5: Track a Donation From the Time it Arrives in the Mail to When the Thank-you Letter Gets Sent

How do the systems in your office currently work? Whether a donation arrives in the mail or through the internet, what happens next?

◆ Who receives the donation?

◆ Who enters it into your database?

◆ Who generates the acknowledgment or thank-you letter?

◆ How long does this process take from the time a donation arrives to the time the thank-you is mailed?

◆ Are all the letters the same or are any different?

◆ Do some letters get personal notes?

◆ Do any donors get thank-you calls or emails in addition to letters?

If this system is operating effectively and efficiently, there's no need to change it. If you find that letters are taking longer than one week to get out the door, it's time for a system review. Industry standard says that acknowledgment letters should be sent within forty-eight hours of the donation arriving, but I find that one week is more achievable in small development shops.

See Chapter Six for additional details on raising more for your annual fund with direct mail.

Step 6: Plan a Board Retreat

When was the last time your organization held a board retreat? Was fundraising on the agenda? Or was it all strategic planning? Be sure to include strategic planning and development (fundraising) on the agenda of all future board retreats.

If your board has not had a retreat (half- or full-day meeting with a different agenda than a regular board meeting) in the last year, it's time to plan one.

If possible, the retreat should be held outside of the organization's normal meeting space and utilize an outside facilitator. To save money, the retreat could be held in a board member's office.

I facilitate a lot of board retreats and witness remarkable, positive changes in board members' attitudes toward fundraising. Here's a great activity for your next board retreat:

In pairs or small groups, have board members practice telling one another why they first decided to volunteer with your organization and why they continue to do so. This powerful exercise will help them become more comfortable talking about your organization in the office and at social events.

Having board members be good advocates isn't about them remembering every statistic about your organization. Nor is it about them memorizing your mission statement. What you want board members to do is communicate their excitement about the organization to everyone they meet. Staff members can fill in the details about the organization at a later date as appropriate and necessary.

to do

If you can't afford to pay a professional facilitator, consider swapping executive directors or development directors with other organizations to lead your retreat.

Board retreats are opportunities for planning and training. Be sure to include components of both on your agenda. At the retreat, it is a time for strategic plans to be created or reviewed as well as to provide governance and fundraising training. Many organizations are super-focused on the planning components and neglect the opportunity for training. An annual board retreat is an important part of a well-functioning board. Plan one with your board chair today.

Step 7: Develop a Plan

Whether you've been at an organization for ten years or you're just arriving and need to create a development office from scratch, you need a plan for how you will raise money this year. A basic plan will have goals, timelines, deadlines, and tasks.

Chapter Four will cover how to create a plan. For now, the important thing to know is that you need one. If you've been operating without a plan, it's never too late to create one.

Step 8: Say Thank You

One of the top reasons that donors cite for not making a second gift to an organization is that they weren't thanked properly or told how their gift was used.

You worked hard to get the first gift and if you don't follow up after the gift is made, then you're going to have to start at the beginning again next year. Getting a new gift is always more challenging than getting a renewal gift from a repeat donor. As long as you have thanked your active donor adequately, you significantly increase your chances of receiving subsequent gifts.

Create a follow-up plan for donors. Start with the basics— everyone gets a thank you letter within one week of making the gift. You should send another letter in six to ten months letting them know how their gift was used.

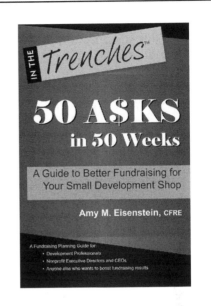

If you want more information on creating a fundraising plan that will lead you to raise more money and truly jump-start your development shop, check out my book, *50 A$ks in 50 Weeks: A Guide to Better Fundraising for Your Small Development Shop.*

Stewardship plans can be simple or extremely complicated. Here are some things you might want to consider when creating your stewardship plan:

◆ Do you have the capability (technology and/or staff capacity) to send a different letter to first-time donors than the one you send to repeat or returning donors?

◆ Are large donors thanked in the same or different ways than smaller donors?

◆ How are online donors thanked?

◆ What is the amount at which donors receive thank-you calls and hand-written notes? Who calls and writes to these donors?

◆ How can you involve the executive director and board members in the thank-you process?

◆ How and when will you let donors know how their gifts were used?

Depending on the size and capacity of your staff and infrastructure, you might not be able to do all of these. Pick and choose the ones that seem manageable, but still adequately thank your donors.

Eight Simple Steps to Create an Outstanding Development Office or Supercharge the One You Have

1. Recruit a new board or meet your existing one. Meet with each board member to discuss the member's interests and involvement.

2. Identify and meet your best donors.

3. Visit your website, make a donation.

4. Create calendars for grants and mailings.

5. Track a donation.

6. Plan a board retreat—schedule one today.

7. Develop a plan.

8. Say thank you.

 practical tip

Do not skip this important step. Follow-up is critical to running a successful fundraising program.

Final Thoughts

It doesn't matter whether you're starting from scratch or working to improve the development office you have; if you follow these eight simple steps, you and your development shop will be off to a strong start!

I recently met with the executive committee of my child's PTO (Parent Teacher Organization). One parent expressed her fear of asking people she knows for money. While I understand her hesitation, the only way to raise money is to ask for it. Ask for it by telling your story and communicate your passion about the organization and cause. Try to identify the potential donor's passion for the cause as well. After you ask, remember to say thank you and be gracious, regardless of whether or not you get the gift. That's what fundraising is really all about; it all comes down to "the ask." It's as simple as that.

To Recap

◆ Fundraising starts with your board members. Talk to them about what they can do financially and how they wish to get involved with fundraising. Plan an annual board retreat for planning and fundraising purposes.

◆ Understand what you've done in the past with regard to fundraising and make a plan for how you will proceed.

◆ Identify how donations are made and how they are tracked. Step into the donor's shoes by making a donation online and learn how the donor is really treated.

◆ Saying thank-you to donors multiple times and in multiple formats is an important part of the fundraising process.

Chapter Two

Fundraising Basics: More Than Odds and Ends

IN THIS CHAPTER

---→ Learn the four stages of the fundraising cycle.

---→ Understand how each stage plays an important part in the overall fundraising process.

---→ Learn the language of fundraising.

---→ See examples of fundraising pyramids and ladders and discover their meaning.

This chapter is a mixture of important information. It lays the groundwork of fundraising processes and systems, and provides you with an important foundation for being a dynamo fundraiser.

There are four steps or stages to the fundraising cycle, and understanding them is critical for success. Your goal is to take each donor through the four stages. Once someone is a donor, your job is to continue to take the person through the cycle repeatedly.

Identification—identifying prospective donors. This could be individuals, corporations or foundations.

Cultivation—building relationships with those potential funders.

Solicitation—asking for a gift (in person, by mail, or with a grant application).

Stewardship—showing gratitude (follow-up and thank you process).

Identification is the first stage of the fundraising cycle. It is where you identify individuals, grant makers, corporations, or other potential donors for your organization.

Cultivation is the second stage of the fundraising cycle, and means "relationship building" in the world of fundraising. This is when prospective donors and representatives of an organization (board and staff members) get to know one another. During cultivation, a prospective donor learns about the organization and the organization's board and staff members gets to know the potential donor.

Solicitation is the third stage of the fundraising cycle and is the actual "ask" or request for money (also referred to as a donation, contribution, or gift). I will use the term to refer to any request for funds, including a grant application, event invitation, appeal letter, sponsorship request, or individual, face-to-face ask.

Stewardship is the final stage of the fundraising cycle and is the thank-you process with a donor after a gift is received. The thank you is an important part of fundraising and should be conveyed multiple times, in multiple ways. Sending thank-you letters, handwritten notes, calls from board members or the director, listing in a newsletter or annual report, and acknowledgment in-person or at an event are all appropriate ways to thank a donor.

A **Prospect** is an individual, foundation, or corporation who has been identified as a potential donor for your organization.

These definitions are repeated in Chapter Seven for the reader who has decided to skip around and not read straight through. Understanding these concepts is critical for successful fundraising, which is why they are worth repeating.

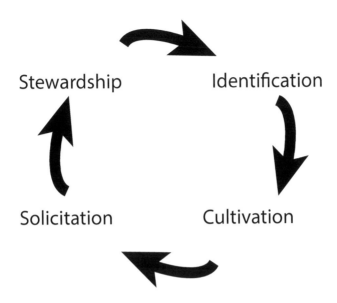

Stewardship   Identification

Solicitation   Cultivation

I will go through each stage of fundraising in more detail in later chapters, but for now, it's important to understand that the stages exist and that moving a funder methodically through the cycle will ensure long-term fundraising success.

Asking Isn't Everything

In the previous section I outlined the four stages of fundraising. The *Fundraising Cycle* pie chart on the following page provides an idea of how much time each stage should take throughout the process. You must go through each stage, whether it takes a year, a month, or a day to complete the cycle.

For example, if it takes ten months to identify, cultivate, solicit and steward a donor, then you will spend approximately one-and-a-half months (15 percent of the time) identifying the person, five months (50 percent of the time) building the relationship prior to asking, then ask (the shortest part of the process—either one moment in time or up to two weeks to give you an answer), and then thank the person over a period of three months (30 percent of the time).

Of course, fundraising is more of an art than a science when it comes to working with people, so do what feels natural, and don't feel any need

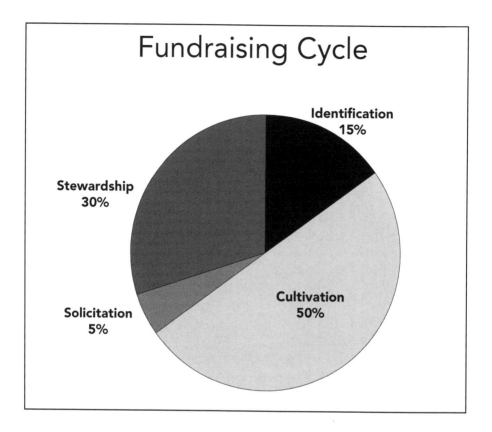

Fundraising Cycle

Identification 15%

Stewardship 30%

Solicitation 5%

Cultivation 50%

to stick to the time frames presented. They are just used to give you an example of how a fundraising process might look.

The part of the fundraising process that people usually fear the most is the solicitation stage, or the actual ask. When people say they don't want to fundraise, *asking* is generally the part they are referring to. However, most people don't know there are other aspects of fundraising. In reality, solicitation (asking) is only a short, although extremely important, part of the process.

This fundraising cycle would be used in any type of solicitation, whether asking for a grant, individual solicitation for the annual fund, or major gift for a capital campaign.

If board members and other volunteers are uncomfortable or afraid to help with asking, you can get them involved with the other 95 percent of the process. They can:

◆ Help identify prospective donors by introducing their friends, family members and colleagues to your organization.

◆ Help build relationships (cultivate) with prospective donors by bringing them on tours of your organization, meeting with them over coffee, or inviting them to a special event.

◆ Help thank donors in person, by sending a note, or making a thank you phone call.

While you want board members engaged in all stages of the fundraising cycle, including the ask (solicitation), some just won't ever feel comfortable doing so. It's better to have them involved in 95 percent of the process, as opposed to none, if all emphasis is placed on the ask.

Change Your Language

One of the reasons I've found that people don't like fundraising is they feel like they're begging, when in reality it's not (or shouldn't be) like begging at all. There's no arm twisting either. Done properly, fundraising is about matching an individual (or couple or family) with a cause they are interested in, and getting them to invest in that cause. When someone invests in the community, the person is making an impact and leaving a mark on the world. It's up to you to inform the donor how the "investment" is doing and provide a "tangible" return on the investment.

Moving Donors Up

One of the goals of any good fundraising program is to move donors up a donation pyramid or ladder. Donors often begin their financial relationship with organizations by making small gifts. If they are thanked and acknowledged and feel that their money was put to good use, they will often make another, larger donation.

Donors generally start giving because a friend asks them to or they receive a solicitation in the mail or by email. It's the job of the development program through cultivation and solicitations to move donors up the pyramid.

Donor Pyramid

Note: Dollar amounts are only used as examples and could be more or less, depending on the current pyramid at your organization.

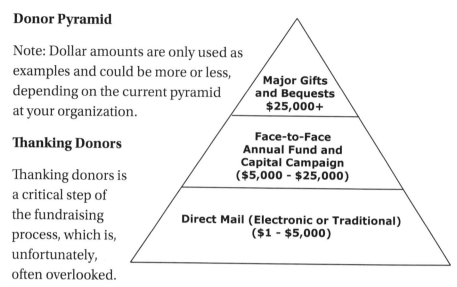

Major Gifts
and Bequests
$25,000+

Face-to-Face
Annual Fund and
Capital Campaign
($5,000 - $25,000)

Direct Mail (Electronic or Traditional)
($1 - $5,000)

Thanking Donors

Thanking donors is a critical step of the fundraising process, which is, unfortunately, often overlooked. I know too many organizations that skip this step because they don't have the staff or time to do it. Inevitably, this becomes a vicious cycle, because they don't have any capacity to fundraise, but then they lose their donors because they aren't thanking them. You get the picture.

If you have the time to ask people for money, then you must take the time to thank them.

The Team Approach to Fundraising

Fundraising is truly a team sport, but unfortunately many people are trying to go it alone. Building your team will be one of the keys to your success. Your team consists of a dedicated executive director, fundraising staff, and board members. Each has a role to play, although roles are often blurred, depending on a variety of factors. Below is the best-case scenario—something to aim for. As your organization grows and matures, roles will naturally shift and change.

Executive Director

The executive director is the "face" and the visionary of the organization. Donors, especially major donors, will want and expect to meet with the executive director before making any significant gift. The executive director will need to be able to communicate the vision of the organization, and convince donors that they are capable of carrying it

A few years back I worked with a cancer research and support organization to help it create a development plan and systems, as well as hire its first development director. The executive director founded the organization to help find a cure for a specific type of cancer his wife had. When he told the story of how his wife survived cancer, you couldn't help wanting to give. Thinking about the story still brings tears to my eyes.

When talking about this organization, the executive director tells you that his wife had been through chemo, radiation, multiple surgeries and more. All of it was unsuccessful, and she was dying. He had been doing research to help her and ultimately came across a clinical trial in which she was able to enroll. Several months later, she was cancer-free (and still is, almost ten years later).

The reason that the story is so powerful is that the executive director owns it and has a clear vision for finding a cure for cancer. Period. No ifs, ands or buts about it. He is so convincing that he will find a cure, that you want to make sure you are a part of it.

Every nonprofit needs its "why us" story and the executive director needs to be able to tell it to everyone and anyone.

stories from the real world

out. The executive director should ask donors for donations in the event that board members are unable or unwilling to do so.

Development Staff

In a small development shop, the development director's job is to coordinate and oversee the execution of all fundraising efforts as well as to drive marketing and public relations efforts. This hefty job description often includes: writing grants, planning events, writing appeals, compiling the annual report, preparing development reports for the board, maintaining the website and social media efforts, and writing newsletters and other PR and marketing pieces. All of this is accomplished far better with the help of support staff, the executive director, and involvement of board members.

Development staff members are responsible for keeping on track with the development plan and helping the executive director move donors through each stage of the fundraising cycle. The director of development is responsible for working with the development committee of the board as well as other board members on fundraising.

To help the executive director and fulfill the development role, the development director should prepare a short list of tasks for the executive director each week. Things on the list might include:

I had the good fortune to work with a social justice organization several years back. One of the board members, who really understood the need for fundraising, was more than happy to do what he could. As a staff member, I provided him with concrete, doable tasks each month. Sometimes the list was to make three thank you calls. Other times it was to schedule an appointment with a potential donor and meet with the person. Left on his own, he didn't know much about fundraising, but was always willing to take guidance and direction. Thanks to him, we raised tens of thousands of dollars which we wouldn't have raised without his involvement and engagement.

stories from the real world

- ◆ Call Tom Smith to thank him for his gift (provide information about the gift and Tom's giving history).

- ◆ Sign the attached ten thank you letters and add personal notes.

- ◆ Contact Judy Jones to schedule a time to get together for coffee within the next three weeks. (Provide background on Judy and the reason for the meeting.)

Fundraising Readiness Checklist

❏ Make certain that the staff and board leadership at your organization understand the fundraising cycle and process.

❏ Review the team approach to fundraising with staff and board leadership at your organization. Determine ways each team member can become more active and engaged.

❏ Design a fundraising pyramid for your organization. Create a strategy for moving donors up your pyramid.

Many states (and D.C.) require charities to register before they solicit donations. Typically you register with the attorney general or secretary of state in the state(s) where you're soliciting. Google "charity registration" and the state name and you can usually find your way from there.

to do

Often, the development director also cultivates relationships with donors and ask for gifts, either to assist the executive director and board president, or because those individuals are unable or unwilling to take on the responsibilities of fundraising.

Board Members and Other Volunteers

Their volunteer status makes board members the most appropriate people to solicit donations. They can ask from a position of being a dedicated volunteer—not being paid by the organization, but believing it's important enough to give their own time and resources.

Board members should be advocates for the organization, actively networking and constantly trying to introduce new "friends" and prospective donors to the organization.

Depending on where your organization is in terms of budget and staff, the roles as I have described them will be close to how your organization operates, or only a fantasy. As you grow, the roles will become clearer and better defined. When you are a new and small organization, it's more of an "all hands on deck" approach and roles will be less defined.

To Recap

◆ Fundraising has four important stages. They are identification, cultivation, solicitation and stewardship. Be sure to move your donors through each stage as quickly and as effectively as possible.

◆ Move donors up the fundraising pyramid. Bring them into your organization through direct mail or events. Cultivate and steward them so they become larger donors for your annual campaign. Hopefully with enough time, attention, and engagement, they will become major donors to your campaigns or through planned gifts.

◆ Fundraising is a team effort, and each member of the fundraising team plays an important role. Your fundraising efforts will be most successful when the executive director, development staff, and board members all work together.

Chapter Three

Building the Fundraising Board of Your Dreams

IN THIS CHAPTER

···➤ The roles and responsibilities of board members, especially with regard to fundraising.

···➤ How to recruit and retain outstanding board members.

···➤ How to have fantastic board meetings.

···➤ How to turn your board members into fabulous fundraisers.

Very often board members are recruited to serve on a board without any expectation of having to make a donation or help with fundraising. Unfortunately, this causes confusion among staff and board members when issues around fundraising arise.

Board members have three primary responsibilities:

◆ Governance and policy making

◆ Fiduciary responsibility and fundraising

◆ Advocacy

For the purposes of this book, we will focus on fundraising, but you should understand that board members have other critical roles to play as well. Often, board members act as though their only role is governance. In other cases, board members are overly involved in day-to-day management of the organization, which is really the responsibility of the executive director.

As I've mentioned in prior chapters, board member roles and responsibilities develop and change as an organization matures. Here are some tasks that board members should not be involved with as long as there are staff members to handle the issues:

◆ Day-to-day management

◆ Programmatic operations

◆ Personnel matters (other than with the executive director)

That said, the role of board members at small or start-up organizations often looks very different than the role of board members at well-established, larger organizations.

Building Your Dream Board

If you're new to fundraising, you might not have known that you should be dreaming about board members, but those of us who have been working with boards for many years know that great board members are more valuable than gold. They can bring resources and networks, as well

I once worked with a small environmental organization on improving its fundraising. It quickly became clear that the board was involved in the day-to-day management of the organization—including weeding the yard around the building and taking out the trash!

Typically, this is NOT something that board members would engage in, but in order to keep the building functional with its limited budget and small staff (one full-time and two part-time persons) it was necessary for board members and other volunteers to engage in these tasks, which would normally be assigned to a staff member. My job was to help grow its fundraising substantially enough to be able to afford to pay someone to help with some of the operational tasks of running the organization.

as a level of trustworthiness and authority to your organization that could rarely be achieved without them.

Board members are an integral part of the fundraising process. Your board members are the closest people to your organization. They are passionate about your mission and your cause, they understand your programs and services, and they know what your budget is and where the gaps in services are. If you can't convince these people to give, how could you convince anyone else? And, why should anyone else give if your board members won't?

There's an expression in fundraising called "give or get." Traditionally it has meant that board members need to help with fundraising by either giving or getting (fundraising). As of now, I'm officially changing this expression to give AND get. This means that board members should give their own contribution as well as help with fundraising. It's not "either/or." It's "and."

100 Percent Participation

One hundred percent participation refers to when every board member makes a personal contribution to the organization. Full participation (every board member giving) is so important to fundraising success because it's extremely difficult to ask someone for money if you haven't made a gift yourself.

In addition, many foundations require 100 percent participation of your board before they will consider a grant. After all, if your own board members won't invest in your organization, why should the foundation? Once you understand how important it is to have 100 percent board participation, the question becomes how to achieve it.

> There's an expression in fundraising that is used with regard to board members called **give and get**. "Give" indicates that board members should each make a personal, financial contribution. "Get" means that each board member should help with fundraising. In other words, "get" funding for the organization

The first step to achieving 100 percent participation is to recruit board members in the first place with an expectation that they will give. Second is to have a board member expectation form which is reviewed with each board member annually.

If you do not already have 100 percent participation from board members, then it should be your number one goal this year. Make this a top priority.

I speak frequently with staff members who are frustrated by non-giving board members. My first question to them is: did you ask? And, how did you ask? If board members are only asked when they are together as a group, it's not good enough.

I worked for a social justice organization that was originally funded by a single individual. This founding funder recruited many of his high-profile friends for the board, with the understanding that he was funding the organization and that they would not need to raise money. However, the organization was wildly successful and outgrew the founder's resources in a relatively short period of time (less than five years). This left the board and executive director, who had also been recruited without an expectation of fundraising, in a challenging situation.

Once the board and executive director realized that they would indeed need to fundraise if the organization was going to continue to grow, they hired their first development director. Although they were slow to get going (it always takes time to change a culture of any organization) the board members did come to understand the fact that they needed to make personal contributions and help with fundraising if they wanted the organization to continue. Fortunately, the board was comprised of high profile people and, as a result, it wasn't extremely difficult to make the transition from a non-fundraising board to a fundraising one!

stories from the real world

Ideally, board members should be solicited by the board president, or development committee chair person, or both. They should be solicited individually and in-person every year. Asking each board member to fill out a board member expectation form at the beginning of each year is a useful way to start the conversation. (See Board Member Expectation form later in this chapter.)

Also, you will want to include board member giving in your board member job description, so board members understand this requirement at the outset.

You will come across board members who believe that they are giving their time and, therefore, do not need to give their money. That is simply untrue. Their time cannot pay the light bills, rent, or staff salaries. When you have a board member who doesn't want to give, it's important to have a serious conversation with the member. See if you can change the member's mind and attitude about giving or help this person find another volunteer position with your organization. Make it clear that giving is a requirement for serving on your board.

What Counts as Participation?

I am often asked if gala ticket purchases count towards board member participation. My answer is yes—and no. Preferably, you want board members buying gala tickets AND contributing to your annual fund. However, if you need to count gala tickets this year to achieve 100 percent participation, while you work on educating board members about the need for a general annual fund contribution from everyone, then go ahead.

What about gifts-in-kind? Gifts-in-kind are donations of time (services) and goods, rather than money. As I mentioned before, gifts-in-kind don't pay the electric bill, rent, or salaries. Occasionally, gifts-in-kind will replace an existing budget line item, such as new computers, furniture, or accounting fees, so you might be more inclined to count them. I'm not talking about goody bags for your gala, but things that you would have purchased anyway as part of your existing budget. Therefore, I'll say that all rules have exceptions, but in general, gifts from board members should be monetary, not just in-kind gifts.

How Much Should Board Members Give?

This question often comes up whenever I work with nonprofit boards. My answer is always the same: board members should give a significant and meaningful gift for their particular budget and situation. This could be one-hundred dollars for some board members and one-hundred thousand dollars or more for others.

Some boards have minimum-gift requirements. There are pros and cons to having a set amount. One advantage of having a set minimum amount is having a crystal clear expectation. Some disadvantages are that board members who can't give the minimum often drop off the board, even if they are otherwise important members. Alternatively, board members who could give more might not, because they have done what they were asked to do.

A good rule of thumb is that board members consider your organization in their top three charities for giving (hopefully in the number one or two slot, but at least third). If members are giving one-thousand dollars to their church and the local hospital, they should be giving that amount or more to your organization as well.

Peer-to-Peer Fundraising

One of the reasons board members are such effective fundraisers is that they can engage in peer-to-peer fundraising. Peer-to-peer fundraising is when one friend or colleague solicits another. It is so valuable because of an existing and equal relationship between the solicitor and the person being solicited. For example, a CEO of one company can often easily solicit the CEO of another, because they both share the same experience and status. Also, in peer-to-peer fundraising, the cultivation process is partially done before you start because there is an existing relationship, and trust a factor between the two.

Another context and example is a bike-a-thon or run. The success of these events depends on participants soliciting their friends and family members. This type of peer-to-peer solicitation is extremely effective, because it's so difficult to say "no" to a friend.

Steps to Building Your Board

Depending on whether you are working with an existing board or creating a new one, you will face different challenges, but the overall process is the same. If you are working with an existing board that needs improvement, follow the same steps as for creating a new one.

As I write this book, I'm currently in the middle of working on a $10 million capital campaign for a school. It's campaign chair is the CEO of an extremely well-known company. His passion for the school, which his son attends, permeates everything he does. He is happy to share the story with all his friends and colleagues and eagerly asks them for gifts for the campaign. Since he hangs around with other CEO's (his peers), they all have the capacity to make a contribution, and many of them have done so. Without his passion and enthusiasm for the campaign and a willingness to ask, we would not have raised nearly as much as we have.

stories from
the real world

The main difference between creating a new board and improving the one you have is that it might be challenging to remove difficult or absentee board members. This is especially true if you don't have the full cooperation of the board president or executive director. Utilize your board-member job description and expectation form to make a case for holding board members to high standards.

Step 1: Create a Board Member Job Description

Board member job descriptions are important tools to use when recruiting new board members. They can also be used to help clarify board member roles and responsibilities with current board members.

The number one complaint from nonprofit staff members that I hear is that board members don't do what they committed to do. One reason is that board members don't fully understand what their responsibilities are. In order to have a good working relationship, it's important that both board and staff members understand what the responsibilities and expectations of board members are. These can be explained and outlined in a good board member job description.

Another reason that board members don't do what they committed to, is that they are busy and stressed. It's your job to communicate with your

Here is a sample board member job description. Feel free to use it as is or tweak it for your organization.

Board members at XYZ organization are the volunteer leaders of the organization and are responsible for the governance, finances and overall well-being of the organization.

Board members are expected to:

◆ Attend meetings and participate in discussions

◆ Provide professional expertise as appropriate and necessary

◆ Serve on at least one sub-committee

◆ Make a significant, personal financial contribution

◆ Serve as good advocates for the organization in the community

◆ Attend organization events (fundraising and otherwise)

◆ Assist with fundraising in a variety of ways

example

board members so that you understand what they are and are not able to commit to. In an effort to be respectful of their time, you should provide easy-to-follow instructions and small, manageable tasks.

Step 2: Create Board Member Expectations

A board member expectation form or agreement is a simple document which is reviewed and signed by each board member annually. This shows what each board member is committing to do each year. The expectation form should be used as a tool to evaluate board members' performance, based on what they said they would do.

BOARD MEMBER EXPECTATION FORM

Name:_____

I understand my financial commitment is necessary to ensure the success of XYZ Organization.

My company (firm) and/or I will participate in the following ways this year:

❑ Dinner Gala ($100/ticket; sponsorships from $500-$10,000) $ _____

❑ Golf ($200/ticket; sponsorship opportunities from $500-$5,000) $ _____

To achieve 100% participation of the board, I personally pledge: $ _____

TOTAL $ _____

For my personal gift, I would prefer to make

❑ One payment   ❑ Quarterly payments of $ _____

❑ My company will match my donation (I will submit the matching gift form with my payment(s)).

Please make gift or first pledge payment by January 31, so we can start the year with 100% participation.

As a board member, I agree to serve on the following committee(s) this year (check all that apply):

❑ Fundraising   ❑ Dinner Gala   ❑ Finance

❑ Golf   ❑ Governance   ❑ Nominating

I would like to help with donor identification, cultivation, stewardship (check all that apply):

❑ Host an informational event in my home.

❑ Make thank-you calls to donors (from home or office—10 calls per year).

❑ Add personal notes to solicitations and thank-you letters (in XYZ office 4 times per year).

❑ Bring colleagues, friends and family to fundraising and cultivation events.

❑ Add 5 or more new names to our mailing list as potential volunteers or donors.

I understand that board meeting attendance is key to the success of the board and the agency and is a requirement for board membership.

Board Member Signature _____ Date _____

example

*Step 3: Create Board Structure
and Committee Descriptions*

One question I'm frequently
asked when working with board
members is: how many board
members should we have?
My answer is, enough to have
an adequate governing body
and structure with populated
committees. If you have seven
board members and four
committees, then you clearly
don't have enough members to
fill all the committee roles.

It is good to have a few
non-board members on
your committees, but each
committee should have at
least some board members on
it. I usually favor boards with
seventeen to twenty-one board members. Any number below fifteen is
too small, because there aren't enough people to fill out committees.

> Board members are volunteers
> and have careers and families
> in addition to volunteering for
> your organization. Be respectful
> of their time and have realistic
> expectations. Attendance at
> one meeting and making calls
> or signing letters is generally a
> reasonable amount of work for
> an average month. Of course,
> some months will be more and
> others less, but make sure that
> you are respectful of their other
> commitments.

 practical tip

Generally small and/or new nonprofits err on the side of having too few
board members versus too many. If you are concerned about having
too many, twenty-five is probably the upper limit, because it's hard to
manage so many people. The primary reason to have at least fifteen or
more board members is so you have a group of people with a wide range
of skills and networks. Also, a larger board means there are more people
to donate and help with fundraising.

Here is a list of some common board committees you might want to
consider for your board.

- ◆ Executive Committee

- ◆ Governance Committee

◆ Fundraising/Development Committee

◆ Investment and Budget Committee

◆ Nominating Committee (Board Member Recruitment)

Step 4: Develop a List of Desired Skills, Attributes, Characteristics and Connections

When thinking about building a board, you want to consider the skills, attributes, characteristics, and connections that would serve your organization well. Below is a list to get you started:

◆ Lawyer

◆ Accountant

◆ PR/Marketing

◆ Human resources

◆ Information technology

◆ Governance

◆ Social media

◆ Professional in the field of service (social worker, physician, etc.)

◆ VP or higher (CEO) at major corporation

◆ Community leader

◆ Philanthropist

◆ Diversity (race, ethnicity, religion, gender, geography)

Obviously, one member could cover more than one category. For example, you could recruit a lawyer from the biggest firm in town, who lives in a county not already represented on your board.

Step 5: Recruiting Board Members

Once you have determined what you would like board members to do (board member job description and expectations) and who you need on your board (list of skills and characteristics) then you are ready to start recruiting. For an existing board, check off the list the characteristics and attributes already filled by current board members. Share your list of desired skills and characteristics with current staff and board members, as well as your volunteers, so they can recommend potential board member candidates.

Prospective board members should be asked to submit resumes and a few sentences on why they are interested in joining your board. A nominating committee should screen candidates and make recommendations to the full board. Once approved, nominees should be asked to join the board. The process should include an interview with the candidate, who should be told the responsibilities and requirements of serving on your board (see *Board Member Job Description and Expectations* form earlier in this chapter). Prospective board members are often invited to attend one board meeting before officially joining the board, as a final step to make certain that they are a good match and fit with the group dynamic.

Step 6: Create Board Member Orientation

Boards would operate much more smoothly if board members were recruited and oriented properly. New board members should learn about the organization by being provided with materials including annual reports, audits, bylaws, brochures, and videos. They should also take a tour of the organization. The executive director and top development staff member should take time to get to know new board members individually to learn their motivation for serving, time commitment and availability, interest in specific committees, connections, knowledge and understanding of fundraising, and more.

Step 7: Hold Great Board Meetings

One of the keys to successful boards is having great board meetings. Unfortunately, most board meetings are so boring that people with busy lives never want to attend. You will need to make attending meetings worth their time and a valuable experience or your board members won't want to come. No one wants to attend a meeting to listen to report after report, especially after a long day at the office.

Instead of reading reports at your board meetings, send reports to members in advance and ask them to come with questions. Discuss only action items that need votes, clarification or fleshing out, rather than simply reporting out.

Here are some ways you can make your board meetings outstanding:

◆ Utilize your board members' skills and talents. Have meaningful discussions by including topics for discussion on the agenda. Ask for their advice and opinions. Don't just use meetings as an opportunity to read reports.

◆ Allow time for networking and socializing. One of the advantages of being on a board for many people is to meet and network with new people. Also, it's difficult to work on committees with people you don't know.

◆ Have nametags (or table tent cards) at each meeting to help attendees get to know one another.

◆ Have a mission moment. Remind board members why they love your organization by tugging at their heartstrings at every opportunity. At each meeting, read a letter from a client, invite a client to provide a testimonial, or show a video to reinforce the importance of your mission and your work.

◆ Provide food. Although it may seem ridiculous to some and obvious to others, it's important to feed your board members—at least a snack and drinks—regardless of the time of your meetings. They are volunteers and are giving up a part of their day to be with you. You don't know what other meetings, work, etc. they are running from (or to) and might not have time to have a snack or a meal. You want them to be fresh and happy at your meeting and providing food is a simple way to accomplish this.

Step 8: Keep Board Members Engaged and Energized

Keep board members engaged and energized by providing them with important, meaningful work to do. Utilize them for their skills, expertise and experience. For example, tell board members what challenges you are facing as an organization and ask them to come up with three possible solutions.

Step 9: Show Gratitude

Show appreciation for what board members do, and they'll want to do more. Throughout the year, remember to thank board members by taking them out to lunch or writing a special thank-you note. Make sure they know you value their contribution (financial and otherwise).

Step 10: Hold Annual Board Retreats

I can't emphasize enough the importance of holding annual board retreats, which are different from your monthly or regular meetings. A mistake that organizations often make is not recognizing the importance of board retreats. Retreats serve multiple functions, all of which are critical for your future success, including:

◆ Reenergizing, motivating, and creating enthusiasm

◆ Planning—creating a strategic plan or reviewing the existing one

◆ Fundraising training

◆ Team building

◆ Assessing and evaluating of the effectiveness of the organization

Boards get formed in a variety of ways, but often begin with a small group of the founding executive director's friends. Most board members are recruited with no expectations of making a contribution or helping with fundraising, or any other requirements. Once this happens, it is difficult to change the culture of the board, but it can and must be done as the organization grows and has new needs and responsibilities.

A Note for National Organizations

When board members are spread out geographically, meeting in-person can be challenging. Plan on having an in-person retreat once a year and budget for it. Ask board members to cover their travel expenses. If possible, offer to cover one night hotel stay and meals. Hold a two-day meeting and then hold monthly or quarterly meetings by conference or video call.

At a local mentoring program, the board was comprised of former mentors, social workers, and other do-gooders in the community. They understood conceptually that they needed to fundraise, but didn't know where to begin and primarily left the work to the executive director and the development director. After a few months of coaching at board and development committee meetings, we were able to transform the board members into fantastic fundraisers and advocates for the organization.

For example, one board member, whom we'll call Joe, had never thought to ask his friends before. Once given the proper tools and encouragement, Joe sent letters on behalf of the organization to a few friends. One of Joe's friends made a donation of $10,000. Yes, not all board members have friends with resources like that, but if you don't ask, you won't get. Joe's friend had been there all along, but Joe had never thought to ask him until I showed him how.

Another example, from the same organization: Another board member went to a local grocery store chain to ask for its help. The store committed to catering the annual picnic for the kids, their families, and the mentors, saving the organization over one-thousand dollars. It was as simple as taking the time to ask.

stories from the real world

To Recap

- ◆ Board members should help with fundraising by making their own contribution as well as helping with each stage of the fundraising cycle.

◆ Recruit and retain great board members by having a good job description, clear expectations, adequate training, exciting meetings, and annual board retreats.

◆ Keep board members energized about your organization by including mission moments at each board meeting.

◆ Utilize your board members' expertise by engaging them in meaningful discussions.

Chapter Four

Creating a Fundraising Plan for Success

IN THIS CHAPTER

···➔ How to determine where you've been and where you're going.

···➔ How creating clear goals and action steps will help you raise more money.

···➔ Important components of a plan: what to include.

It's difficult, if not impossible, to know what you've accomplished or if you've been successful if you don't have a plan, with goals, to measure your progress. Having a written development plan is important so that you have a guide to follow. That doesn't mean that you can't change the plan mid-stream, but a plan will tell you where you've been and where you're going.

Creating a development plan can be a quick, simple process; it doesn't have to be complicated or drawn out. There are pros and cons to creating each type of plan (simple or complex), but for a small or new development shop, I recommend the quicker, simpler plan. It will be easier for you to create, follow, and change as appropriate and necessary.

Creating a Baseline

I'm sure you've heard the saying, "if you don't know where you're going, how will you know when you arrive?" Likewise, how would you know if

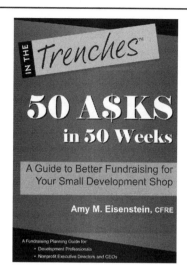

In my book, *50 Asks in 50 Weeks*, I walk readers through how to identify the number of asks that they've made during the past year and count them in each of the following four areas:

◆ Grants

◆ Events/sponsorship

◆ Individual solicitations

◆ Bulk mail

This process helps create a benchmark or baseline, so you know where you've been and can better plan where you want to be.

you've reached your goal if you haven't set any? And finally, how do you know if you've made any progress, if you don't know where you've been? By setting realistic fundraising goals, you can measure your success and celebrate accomplishments. By outlining your achievements, you can know where you've been.

A baseline is your starting place, or what you're doing now. Be sure you know how many grants you're writing and receiving, the number of individuals you solicit each year, how many bulk mail pieces you send and how many donations you receive as a result. Worksheets in this chapter will help create your baseline.

Evaluating Your Fundraising Program

It's important to know not just how much you've raised at the end of the year, but how and why. How much has each project raised (grant, event, individual solicitation, bulk mail effort, social media campaign, etc.)? And, how much did each cost, including staff time?

In order to raise money, you need to understand which fundraising activities and techniques are efficient and

Events—Creating a Baseline

Event Name	Total Ticket Sales	Number Tickets Sold	Gold Sponsors	Silver Sponsors	Bronze Sponsors	Auction Total	Expenses	Gross Income	Net Income
Dinner Gala	$1,000	100	1 @ $5,000 = $5,000	4 @ $2,500 = $10,000	10 @ $1,000 = $10,000	$5,000	$16,000	$31,000	$15,000

effective. That's not to say that every type of fundraising is created equal. Certain types of fundraising take longer initially, but the payout is often significantly higher, such as with planned gifts and other types of fundraising from individuals.

Events

Events, which are probably the most popular way for new nonprofits to raise money, are an enormous amount of work. Of course, events are important to have for a variety of reasons including public relations, profile raising, building your mailing list, raising unrestricted operating revenue, and more. However, events are also the most expensive and labor-intensive type of fundraising. With that in mind, weigh the pros and cons of each of your events. Instead of having three or four (or more) special events per year, narrow it down to one or two of the most lucrative events.

Almost all small- and medium-sized nonprofits that I've worked with are guilty of having too many special events. It's challenging for board and staff members to think about cutting some, but if you are having more than two per year, you should eliminate the least productive in order to invest your time and resources effectively.

Grants

Make a list of grant applications submitted and those actually received, the amount of paperwork required for each, and the amount of the grant. A relatively small grant (five-thousand dollars or less) with lots of requirements and paperwork might not be worth your time and effort.

Grant Applications—Creating a Baseline				
Foundation/ Corporation Name	Amount Requested	Amount Received	Paperwork and Requirements	Reapplication Deadline

Bulk Mail

Evaluate your direct mail program (traditional and electronic mail) by tracking the following:

◆ Number of solicitations sent

◆ Number of donations made

◆ Average gift size

◆ Retention and attrition rates

Compare these numbers from one year to the next to better understand how your program is doing over time, and if it's showing improvement. (See *Bulk Mail—Creating a Baseline* chart on the following page.)

Individual Solicitation

I will leave my discussion of individuals for Chapter Seven, which covers them thoroughly.

SWOT Analysis

A SWOT analysis is a simple, yet powerful and commonly used tool in evaluating and planning. The acronym stands for Strengths, Weaknesses, Opportunities, and Threats. Below is an example of a SWOT analysis I did for a client recently as part of a development plan:

Strengths

◆ Passionate, dedicated executive director

◆ Committed board members

◆ Relationships with foundation funders

◆ Strong, clear mission and programs

Weaknesses

◆ Part-time executive director (should be full-time)

◆ No administrative support

Bulk Mail—Creating a Baseline

Name/ Description	Number Mailed	Number of Gifts Received	Total Raised	Average Gift	High Gift	Low Gift	Notes
Fall Appeal #1	823	105	$4,085	$78	$700	$15	Appeal mailed on October 12, with new brochure.

♦ Confusing and difficult-to-use website

♦ Low income fundraising event

♦ Few current donors and supporters

Opportunities

♦ Increase board size and scope

♦ Develop a signature fundraising event

♦ Grow database of supporters

♦ Create a social media presence

Threats

♦ Economy

♦ Competition from other local nonprofits

♦ Growing pains of being a new organization

As part of your development plan, include a SWOT analysis. It will help you think about and flesh out the areas you need to expand and work on.

Setting Goals

If you are raising funds and setting fundraising goals for the first time, it's an exciting place to be. Your goals will be educated guestimates, and are likely to be off, but that's okay. Aim high. Think big!

How much would you need to accomplish your mission? That should be one factor in setting your goal. I say that because people are limited by their beliefs and due to the misperception that fundraising needs to be difficult. If you think small, that's what you'll raise.

> Goals should be set based on what you actually believe you can raise based on prospective donors and projected income, not the hole or gap in the budget.

practical tip

Most experts say that you should set goals based on your prospects, which is true. However, that goal can be extremely difficult to calculate accurately if the organization doesn't have any prior fundraising data.

If you are at an organization with a fundraising history, you should not set goals simply by adding five percent to what you raised last year. Goals should be set based on what you actually believe you can raise based on prospective donors and projected income, not the hole or gap in the budget. Do this by listing your prospective donors and income from each campaign, including:

- Individual solicitations

- Grants—corporate and foundation

- Events

- Bulk mail (traditional mail and electronic)

Involving Your Board (Getting Buy-In)

Because you will want your board members to help with fundraising, you will want to engage them in the planning process. Depending on the level of involvement of your board members and your development committee members, they can help with the creation of the plan or review and discuss after you have created a first draft.

Plan Contents

- SWOT analysis

- Timeline

- Budget

- Events you will have and how they are going to get accomplished

- Grants to apply for and who is responsible for them

- Individual prospects and who will cultivate and solicit them

♦ Bulk mail schedule with deadlines and themes

♦ Goals

Following Your Plan

The plan is only as good as the people who follow it (or don't). It's useless if it's getting dusty on a shelf. Plan weekly "check-in" meetings to stay on track. You might also consider having a quarterly review session with your development committee. At those meetings, check to find out if you are on track and make adjustments as necessary.

Having an Outside Perspective Can Help

When I am asked to write a development plan for clients, I review their current fundraising efforts and evaluate them based on programs I have

One way I recommend that my clients stay on track is to have a mandatory weekly development meeting. This meeting is with members of the development team (executive director and any development staff, engaged board members, and possibly administrative assistants). If board members are participating, the meeting can take place over the phone. It should not last more than fifteen minutes and should have the same two agenda items every week.

The agenda items for the weekly meeting are:

1. Who did we ask last week?

   How did it go and what's the necessary follow up? Who is responsible for following up?

2. What asks are coming up?

   Who is responsible and what needs to be done to make them happen?

to do

Here are some sample goals for your development plan to get you started.

1.   Expand the board and increase board giving.

Objective A: Diversify the board by adding three to five new board members from various industries, and with skills and characteristics not already represented by (a specific date).

Objective B: Achieve 100 percent participation (every board member writes a personal check, over and above membership dues) by (by a specific date close to the beginning of the year—calendar or fiscal).

Objective C: Expand development committee by adding three to five new members (board and non-board members) and assign each board member at least one task to help with fundraising by (a specific date).

2.   Start an individual giving program.

Objective A: Identify twenty prospects to cultivate this year.

Objective B: Cultivate prospects from your list by inviting them to events, meeting with them at their homes or offices, and providing them with regular updates.

Objective C: Ask your best prospects for donations of a specific amount ($1,000 or more each), in person.

3.   Create a signature fundraising event.

Objective A: Recruit ten board and non-board committee members who have access to potential sponsorships to serve on event committee and determine type and scope of event.

Objective B: Schedule event date and book venue for fall.

Objective C: Solicit ten potential sponsors and plan event.

example

seen at other organizations. I create a section called "recommendations," which are similar to goals, to help them move ahead.

To Recap

◆ Creating a baseline is an important part of the process, so you know where you have been.

◆ There are several strategies for setting goals, but however you set your goals, be sure to write them down so you know when you've accomplished them.

◆ A plan is worthless unless it is followed. Hold a weekly check-in session to keep on track and make adjustments as necessary and appropriate.

Chapter Five

Technology, E-Philanthropy, and Social Media

IN THIS CHAPTER

···→ The important role of technology in fundraising.

···→ How to build your website with donors in mind.

···→ How to start an electronic fundraising program.

···→ The importance of a comprehensive donor database.

···→ The use of social media and your organization.

If you are at one of the many organizations that have not joined the 21st century with regard to technology, then it's time to catch up or close up. In this day and age, there's no excuse for any organization not having:

◆ An up-to-date website.

◆ The ability to send email to supporters.

◆ The ability to accept credit card donations online.

◆ A social media presence.

Without this basic but necessary technology, it will be impossible for you to communicate adequately with supporters or request and obtain donations for your organization. If you can't get your basic technology infrastructure in working order, then how will you operate an effective fundraising program?

Website

The first way that most people will evaluate your organization is via your website, so it needs to be professional and up to date. Almost all prospective donors and volunteers will visit an organization's website before getting involved. This is true of most donors, regardless of whether they intend to make an online donation or actually write a check. Even people who don't give online will visit the website to learn more about your organization.

Your website should have basic information, such as:

To bring your fundraising into the 21st Century, be sure you have the following:

♦ Professional and easy to use website with contact information of the organization and staff members.

♦ A "donate now" button, easily accessible on every page of your website.

♦ Easy to use online donation page.

♦ Ability to send email updates, invitations, and solicitations

♦ Social media efforts and campaigns

to do

♦ How to contact the organization (phone number, address, names, and email addresses for key staff members).

♦ Your mission statement

♦ Descriptions of your programs and services

♦ A "donate now" button on each page of your website

♦ Photos and video

◆ Current listing of events

◆ Volunteer opportunities

◆ Testimonials, quotes

Your website should look attractive, professional, and be easy to navigate. This is the first impression that most donors and prospective donors will have of your organization. If your site is unappealing, you could lose visitors as fast as the click of a mouse.

Here are a few tips for making your website attractive and easy to use:

◆ Keep your web pages clean and uncluttered. This is especially important nowadays, as many people use smart phones to browse the web.

◆ Break up any large blocks of text into smaller, easier-to-read paragraphs and sentences.

◆ Use as little text as possible to get your point across.

◆ Use headings! Remember: people don't read web pages; they scan them. Headings make your pages much easier to scan.

◆ Test your site. Make sure all the links work, your contact form works, and your online donation process works. Nothing screams unprofessional louder than a broken website.

Email

It's important to have an email address for each staff member that utilizes the organization's domain name. Nothing makes me cringe more than getting a business card from someone at an organization with an email address of Hotmail or Gmail. Each staff member should have an email address with the person's name and the domain name of the organization, for example, aeisenstein@nameofyourorganization.org. Keep email addresses as simple and consistent as possible. For example, first initial and last name of the person generally works well.

Having an organizational email address is so important because it shows donors that your organization is legitimate and professional. Would you made a donation based on the request of "amy@gmail.com"?

If you are using Gmail or Hotmail for staff email addresses, STOP. Email addresses/mailboxes should have come with the purchase of your website. Contact your web host to learn how to start using those mailboxes so staff members have their own email address with the name of the organization.

practical tip

Donor Database

Your database plays a critical role in your ability to fundraise successfully. It can help you keep track of donations and it allows you to determine who your best donors are.

If you're just starting to grow your list, I do not recommend spending money on expensive fundraising software. I prefer something reasonably priced or even free! If you already have Microsoft Office Professional Edition, you can use Microsoft Access. Many organizations also use a free-for-nonprofits version of Salesforce at http://www.salesforce.com. There are also many sophisticated donor databases if you are ready to take the next step in growing your established list, including DonorPerfect at http://www.donorperfect.com and a variety of programs by Blackbaud at http://www.blackbaud.com.

Regardless of whether you use an expensive fundraising database or not, your database must be able to capture and store key information, including (but not limited to):

- ◆ Prefix and suffix

- ◆ Name, first and last

- ◆ Contact info (address, phone, email address, etc.)

- ◆ Donation history (how much, when, for which appeal, etc. they have given)

- ◆ Link to your organization (are they friends with a board member?)

- ◆ Notes

You may have heard the expression, "garbage in, garbage out." What you put into the database is what you get out of it. Regardless of whether you have the most sophisticated software or are using something basic, if your data entry is sloppy, then your database won't do you any good. To prevent this, have someone other than the person doing the data entry do spot checks from time to time.

There are many good donor management databases on the market ranging from complex and expensive to relatively inexpensive. Give it your due diligence and research what's available before making a selection. Ask for a list of references for each product you are considering. Call those organizations and ask how long they have been using the product, what they are using it for, what they like and dislike about it, how the initial set-up process was, and how the support is.

Once you have selected a database to track your donors and supporters, you are ready to grow your list and start fundraising!

Electronic Fundraising

Every year, more and more donations are made online. This trend will undoubtedly continue. Therefore, it is critical to include online fundraising in your bag of fundraising tricks.

There are a variety of ways to fundraise electronically. Here are a few to get you started:

◆ Have a "donate now" button on your website.

This button should not only appear on your home page, but on every page of your site. This button should take donors to a secure page where they can enter their credit card information and make a donation immediately, without going to any other pages first. If possible, this page should "look and feel" like your website. This means you should try to avoid having donors go to outside sites like PayPal, if you can avoid it.

◆ Include a "click here to donate" on all electronic communications (top and bottom).

Every time you send an email, you should provide your supporters with an opportunity to give easily and support your programs. Whether you are sending an announcement about an upcoming event, a program update, or online newsletter, you want to enable prospective donors to donate if they wish to. This is called a "soft ask," because there is no specific appeal.

◆ Send electronic solicitations.

In addition to the communications listed above for marketing, be sure to send direct solicitations to your electronic list every year. This solicitation is similar to your mail appeal letters, only in electronic format. However, email solicitations should not simply be your paper solicitations in email format. Keep in mind that people read email differently than letters. Keep them short (one screen, if possible) and include only one link—your "call to action" asking for a donation. If absolutely necessary, you can embed another link to offer more information about your organization.

When your Donate Now button or other online giving alternative goes live, you're deemed to be soliciting in about half the states. It's hard to know exactly how many because lots of state laws haven't kept up with technology. Soliciting triggers state charity registration requirements and you have to register where you solicit even if no one ever makes a gift online—or from a particular state. It's your solicitation reaching the citizens of a given state that often creates the need to register, not the money coming in. An email asking for a gift constitutes a solicitation in most states.

 practical tip

Ask board members and other volunteers to forward emails to their lists. Recipients are much more likely to open emails from friends than they are from organizations. This will help personalize the solicitation and increase chances for response and success.

When you do send bulk email, include a method for subscribers to forward your email to a friend, as well as "opt-out" or get off your electronic mailing list if they wish.

Online Donations

Once potential donors click on the "donate now" button on your website, where does it take them? Do they have any options? Is it easy to make a donation or do they need to navigate through several pages?

If you have never made an online donation to your own organization, stop reading and go make one now.

How do you know how easy or difficult it is for the donor if you've never gone through the process yourself? Here are some additional questions to answer about your online giving process:

◆ Can donors join a recurring giving club or make a monthly gift?

Last December, I went to the website of a local hospital foundation in my area to make a year-end donation. After I filled in my name, address, credit card info, etc., the website prompted me to "log on" before it would complete my transaction. As a first-time user I had to select a username, for which I typed "amyeisenstein." I received an error message and was told that the username was taken. However, before it let me try again, I had to reenter all of my personal and credit card information! I tried again (with a different username) only to have the same thing happen again.

Now I was frustrated. I love this hospital because it's where I had my son and subsequently have taken him for stitches on more than one occasion.

Because I was determined to make the donation, I tried again. Unfortunately, a third attempt failed as well.

I happen to know the development director there, so I sent her off an email asking for help. I can only imagine that a less committed donor would have given up after the second or even first try.

It turns out I wasn't doing anything wrong! Whatever system they use made online donations that difficult!

 stories from the real world

◆ Can donors make a gift "in honor of" or "in memory of" someone?

◆ Can donors make gifts to specific funds or programs?

As discussed above, more and more donors are moving to online giving. Make certain they can do so with ease.

Social Media

Social media, such as Facebook, LinkedIn, Twitter and countless others are an important part of our everyday lives. You will want to take advantage of these modern ways to engage donors and friends for your organization. How much you utilize them will be up to you, but spending fifteen to thirty minutes per day working with social media can be a productive way to engage people and spread your message.

If you are just getting started, you will want to learn about the most popular social sites. Speak with volunteers, board members, interns, or clients who are already active on social media sites. Find out how they would like to interact with your organization online.

Select two sites to begin with, because if you create accounts on more than two, it may become overwhelming and you'll be more likely to neglect them all. Make a commitment to update the two you've selected each day for ten minutes apiece.

If you are unfamiliar with social media, ask an intern or volunteer to help you set up your accounts and get you

---

Social media has unique terminology all of its own. Here are some common terms to get you started:

Post—what you do when adding a comment on many social media sites.

Friend—someone you're connected with on Facebook and other social media sites.

Tweet—a post on Twitter.

Twitter handle—the "@" sign, plus your name or the name of the organization.

Link—you "link" with someone on LinkedIn when you join their network or vice-versa.

(de)finition

Social Media Checklist

❑ Commit to having a social media presence for your organization.

❑ Educate yourself on the available tools and websites by looking at your competitors' websites to see what they are doing. If appropriate, consider asking your kids or younger board members for help in identifying other social sites.

❑ Hold a meeting to devise a plan. Recruit board members or other volunteers that are active with social media for a "getting started" meeting. Make a list of the current, popular social media sites. Consider their strengths and then choose two to start with.

❑ Create accounts and start social media outreach. If necessary, find an intern to help. When creating profiles, pages, and accounts, be sure that the person who has access to the password is authorized to "post" on behalf of the organization. The intern is probably not the most appropriate person to be creating official content for these sites.

For each site you will be required to provide your name, a password, and, when prompted, an image (such as the logo), along with a brief profile which can be an abbreviated form of your mission.

NOTE: After creating your profile on Facebook, you'll need to create a "page" for your organization. You'll want people to connect with your organization's fan page rather than with you personally.

❑ Begin to connect with people by inviting friends and colleagues to connect with you. On Facebook, ask people to "like" your page. With Twitter, you can follow people without them having to follow you back. However, many of them will choose to follow you back.

❑ Set aside twenty minutes per day to update your social sites and engage with supporters. Provide good content about your mission, organization, or cause, which others are more likely to circulate around the web and therefore gain you more exposure. Periodically ask your fans and followers for donations and help.

❑ Hold a monthly call with your committee members to determine strategies and create great content to share on your social sites.

❑ Follow other nonprofits to see what they're doing and sharing. Modify their tactics to suit your cause.

to do

started. Invite your board members, volunteers, and others to "like," "friend," or "follow" you, depending on the site. Add social media links to your website and email correspondence.

When I graduated from college, my grandfather (at the age of 79) bought himself his first computer. He learned to email, keep spreadsheets of his finances, type letters, and surf the web. It was painful for me to watch him "hunt and peck" his way around the keyboard, but he loved it! If he could become computer literate, so can you!

practical tip

When updating your social sites, you might not know what to say. Think about what might be relevant to members of your audience. What would they be inclined to share with others? This could be current information or statistics about your cause, along with other relevant information from articles and blogs that will inform your audience. Feel free to generate some original content too.

Follow the 80/20 rule. Make an effort to provide approximately 80 percent relevant content and 20 percent promotional content. If every update is asking people for something or to do something for your cause, then you won't generate a dialogue and you'll lose a lot of followers and fans.

To Recap

◆ Make sure your organization is competitive in the 21st Century.

◆ Keeping your website looking professional, updated, and easy to navigate is critical for online and off-line fundraising success.

◆ Communicate with donors and supporters by email on a regular basis.

◆ Engage in social media to attract new supporters and interact with current ones.

◆ Accepting donations online is essential to a comprehensive 21st Century fundraising program.

Chapter Six

Building Your Annual Fund with Bulk Mail

IN THIS CHAPTER

···➔ How to build an annual fund through the use of bulk mail—traditional and electronic.

···➔ Why a database is important for your success.

···➔ How to make the most of your bulk mail through personalization.

···➔ Letter writing and response mechanisms.

The annual fund refers to the monies raised to support your annual operations and programs. This chapter combines discussion of annual fund and bulk mail, because a large portion of donors make donations to organizations for the first time through bulk mail. This process can be the bread and butter of an organization's annual fund, if done well.

Why Direct Mail?

Direct mail serves multiple purposes for your nonprofit. First, it serves as a source of ongoing annual revenue, often unrestricted operating revenue. The only exception is if you specify something in an effort to increase donations by having donors give to a specific program or

An **annual campaign** or **annual fund** as it's often called, is an ongoing effort to raise unrestricted and restricted donations for your annual budget and operations. Annual fund campaigns can encompass all efforts to raise funds in a given year, including appeals, fundraising events, grants, and personal solicitations.

service. If you have been at a nonprofit for more than one day, you know that unrestricted revenue is like gold to the organization, because it can be used for anything you need, including traditionally difficult-to-fund budget items such as administrative costs, and your own salary!

Direct mail is also used to build your list of ongoing supporters. This is important and useful, as you will see later on, in terms of identifying your best prospects for individual fundraising (face-to-face) and potential major gifts, capital campaign prospects, and planned gifts, in the future.

For better or worse, direct mail might not raise as much as you spend, or invest (in the program), in the first year. Fundraising efforts can sometimes require an initial investment that doesn't show an immediate return. This can be frustrating and unexpected for many nonprofits. However, I believe it's an investment worth making for a future source of unrestricted operating funds, as well as for the opportunity to move your donors up the gift pyramid.

One reason that mail campaigns can get off to a slow start is that your list of "supporters" will not be accustomed to your asking them for money by mail (snail or electronic mail) so they will need to learn to expect your solicitations before beginning to respond.

Even as a fundraising professional, I am sometimes guilty of neglecting to return envelopes of organizations that I intend to support. Often, it will take receipt of two or three envelopes before I get around to returning one with a contribution. It's important to be persistent and send multiple solicitations to get your program off to a fantastic start.

Read on to learn ways to make sure that even your first mailing is a huge success.

Building Your List

Any strong development program has a long list of supporters and prospective supporters. Whether you have ten people or ten thousand on your list, you will want to grow it with good prospects. If you have a huge list, but it's full of people who aren't interested in your cause or have long ago moved away, it's not a good list, so clean it up. You can clean your list by calling everyone on it to check their information (not very practical), you can pay for an address correction during your next mailing with the post office, or you can hire a professional firm that cleans mailing lists.

Begin building your list by adding friends, family members and colleagues of your staff, board members and other volunteers. Depending on your clientele, you might want to include them. Hospitals, universities, museums, and other organizations like those certainly include clients on their lists of potential supporters. Other organizations, such as homeless shelters and soup kitchens, are less likely to include clients on their lists.

Constantly be on the lookout for ways to grow your lists. Be sure to include everyone who contacts your organization for information as well as all attendees at events.

Unrestricted means that funds can be used for anything required by the budget. There are no restrictions on it.

Restricted means that a donor (or grantor) has limited the use of funds for a specific program, project, or item.

Loyal donors are those donors who support an organization year after year.

Attrition is used to refer to the rate at which donors are lost or "leave" (stop donating).

Retention is used to refer to the rate at which donors are "kept" or continue to donate.

Donor Database

A comprehensive and functional donor database is critical for fundraising success, especially with direct mail. There is a wide range of databases on the market, ranging from inexpensive to expensive. And, expensive doesn't necessarily mean better. I've seen many small nonprofit organizations invest in expensive software that is much too sophisticated for their needs and never use 90 percent of the functions. There's just no need for that type of investment as you grow your list.

Ask other nonprofit professionals in your field (or at similarly sized organizations) what database they use and whether or not they recommend it, and why. If you do decide to invest in fundraising software, find out what type of support the company offers and how long it has been in business. (For a more detailed discussion of databases, see Chapter Five, Technology, E-Philanthropy and Social Media.)

Here is a small sampling of reports that you will want to be able to run easily from your database:

♦ List of your largest donors from the last twelve months. For example, all donors who gave more than one-thousand dollars.

♦ List of cumulative giving. List your largest donors based on their lifetime (cumulative) giving over the last year, or last five years.

♦ List of loyal donors. Anyone who has given more than five times in the last ten years.

♦ All board members with their giving histories and contact information.

♦ All former board members.

♦ Donors who made a gift last year, but haven't made a gift yet this year, known as LYBUNTs—Last Year But Not This (Year).

♦ Event donors, ticket buyers, or sponsors.

♦ First-time donors.

As I will discuss later in the chapter, the more you can segment and otherwise personalize your mailing, the more success you will have. Make sure your database can help you with this as much as possible.

Traditional Mail – Your Appeal and Beyond

Before email, traditional mail was the only form of bulk solicitation. I am using the term traditional mail to mean anything that goes through the post office and needs a stamp. This traditional form of solicitation has been used successfully by organizations for decades and continues to be an important method of fundraising for many organizations. Statistics show that many people, both young and old, still make donations in response to traditional mail solicitations. Therefore, I encourage you to continue your mail program until your online fundraising efforts are doing significantly better than your offline efforts.

Since traditional mail can be extremely expensive for organizations, including postage and printing, I recommend that organizations only mail as many times per year as they can afford. When I use the term "afford" I am referring to time as well as money. Creating a mailing takes time as well as financial resources. Both should be considered when planning your schedule of mailings. To keep your costs down, be sure to trim your lists and only mail to your best prospects.

I recommend sending traditional mail, including both solicitations and marketing pieces, between four and ten times per year. When deciding on a mail schedule, include one or two appeal letters, event invitations, and marketing pieces. For example, two appeal letters, two newsletters and two event invitations. Make a calendar for the year for the bulk mail pieces you will send via traditional mail.

Depending on the size of your mailing list and your budget, you might want to have a mail house handle your mailing or you might handle it in-house.

While many people are inundated with direct mail

LYBUNTs – Last Year But Not This (Year), which means a donor gave last year, but hasn't given yet this year. It's important to renew such donors in order to have a chance of getting donations from them in the future.

SYBUNTs is short for Some Year But Not This (Year). These former donors are harder to renew than LYBUNTs, because they haven't given in over a year, but are easier to get a gift from than non-donors.

pieces, many do respond to organizations that pique their interest and appeal to their needs and desires. It will be important for your direct mail piece to stand out in the proverbial and literal mailbox. How will you get your piece noticed and opened? Don't make the mistake of thinking the outer envelope doesn't matter, because if it goes in the trash before being opened, no matter how good your letter or brochure is, you won't get a donation.

Turning Your Appeals Electric!

Electronic mail has recently taken center stage with regard to fundraising over traditional mail. If you have not yet started communicating with your list of supporters via email, then you are seriously behind the times (as mentioned in Chapter Five). It is critical that your database include email addresses and that you have the capability to send email notifications, solicitations and updates to your list. Your software package should have an interface for mass mailing to enable you to do this easily. As an alternative you can use other services on the market such as Constant Contact.

As discussed in Chapter Five, online appeals are not simply your traditional mail appeals online. Consider how people read email. It should be short and sweet—one screen page, if possible. Use a link (donate button) to drive readers to your online giving page. The subject line must be compelling and thought provoking so the email gets opened in the first place. A subject line reading: "Hi from your local hospital" is neither compelling nor thought-provoking. Neither is "read me." The

In my book, *50 A$ks in 50 Weeks*, when counting solicitations in the category I call bulk mail, I count all bulk mail pieces, including appeal letters, event invitations, newsletters or annual reports with Business Reply Envelopes (BRE's).

most compelling subject line I've ever seen was sent out by Save the Children and read, "Look what YOU did!"

Personalize for Best Results

One key to your success will be how well you personalize your solicitations. You may have heard of the concept of donor-focused fundraising. Donors want to be treated as individuals as much as possible. Bulk mail does not naturally lend itself to this, but it will be up to you to address your donors to the best of your ability. The most effective way to do this is to personalize bulk mail letters, so they feel less "bulky."

Tips for taking the "bulk" out of bulk mail—personalize solicitations as much as possible:

◆ Segment mailings as much as possible and write different letters to donors/non-donors and any other constituent groups you might have. Other examples include LYBUNTs, SYBUNTs, first time donors, etc.

When using a mail house or printer for the first time, be sure to screen carefully:

◆ Ask other nonprofit organizations in your area which vendors they use, how long they have been using them and if they are happy with the service they receive. Ask if they have had any issues with that particular vendor.

◆ Call three or four vendors to discuss your project and get quotes (prices). Ask lots of questions if you don't understand the process. Make sure they break down quotes so you are comparing apples with apples.

◆ Select a vendor to work with. Cheapest is not always best. Sometimes a mid-level vendor is a better choice if the end product and service will be higher quality and on schedule.

practical tip

- ◆ Address donors by name, never "Dear Friend."

- ◆ Hand address outer envelopes to your top donors.

- ◆ Use "live" stamps (not postage meter stamps) on the outside envelopes.

- ◆ Write personal notes on letters, especially if you know the recipient. Have board members write notes to people they know.

Personalize emails too. If you can segment and tailor emails for specific, targeted audiences, you are likely to get a better response. Ideally, have emails sent from board members' email accounts to their friends. Recipients are much more likely to open email from those they know.

Writing the Letter

Contrary to popular belief, appeal letters should be about the donors, not the organization. I know that might not make a lot of sense, but read the following letter and see for yourself.

When writing appeal letters, count the number of times the words "we" and "you" are used. Every time you use the word "we," you are writing about the organization and the focus is no longer on the donor.

Letters should include things such as:

- ◆ Photos

- ◆ Testimonials

- ◆ Personal stories

- ◆ Statistics

- ◆ Accomplishments

- ◆ Gaps in service (what your clients need)

Donor-centric or **donor-focused fundraising** refers to a type of fundraising where the focus is on the donor's needs as opposed to the organization's needs. It's not that the organization needs money, it's that the donor wants to help find a cure for cancer—and the organization is the conduit for fulfilling the donor's wants and needs.

definition

Sample Letter Drafted by One of My Clients

Below is a sample end-of-the-year appeal letter crafted by one of my clients. As you can see, it focuses on the organization rather than the donor. Following the letter are the recommendations I made to improve the letter.

Dear Friends of XYZ Environmental Organization,

As this year comes to an end, we would like you to consider making a special, tax-deductible, end-of-year contribution to the XYZ Organization.

Why, you might ask, should you donate to us?

- Our vision is that fifty years from now, the XYZ environment and river will be as clean and beautiful as it is today. It costs money to do this—to test the river water quality, provide classroom education to kids, and to provide all our programs.

- We are a local nonprofit environmental organization, doing things right here in your own community. Our mission is to "preserve and protect the XYZ River Watershed, including its natural and cultural resources." We are the only organization that truly represents the interests of all the people and communities that live within the watershed.

- We are pragmatic and make decisions based on sound science and data. We are actively involved in the issues. We collaborate with all interested parties.

- We are a well-run organization with outstanding leadership. Our Executive Director, Sally, has been a member of this association since its beginning, and she continues to passionately provide the excellent leadership that has brought us this far.

- We are here to stay. We have been around for nineteen years and the enthusiasm of our trustees, staff and membership is amazing!

We really need your support. If you share in our vision, please consider this end-of-year appeal.

Sincerely,

Board President

P.S. For more information about what we do, please see our website www.xyzorganization.org or call us at XXX-XXXX.

Strengthening the Letter: My Recommendations to the Client

Here were my recommendations for making the letter stronger, more effective, and donor-focused.

◆ The letter is all about you (the XYZ organization). All bullets start with we (or our). Try to focus more on the donor. What will donating do for them? Start some of your bullets with you.... For example, if YOU want the river to be clean and safe for your children and grandchildren to swim and fish in... What do they get out of donating. Why should they care (how does it affect them?)

◆ I'm thrilled to see you have a P.S. that is a "call to action," but it should be a call to donate, not just to visit the website. For example: P.S. Membership dues alone don't cover the cost of keeping the river safe and clear, so make a donation today. You can do so via credit card on our website at www....

◆ Is there any chance you can say, Dear Steve, instead of Dear Friend of XYZ Org? The more you can personalize the letters, the more success you'll have. You shouldn't be sending dear friend letters to your members – you should know who they are (and they should know that you know who they are).

◆ In the "gets things done" bullet, mention something specific. What have you gotten done this year?

◆ Don't be afraid of a two-page letter. If you're putting the mission on the back, then feel free to continue other content there as well. Can you add statistics of what you accomplished this year? Say something interesting about how the hurricane/

floods/other environmental issues affected the river this year and what role you play in that?

How can *you* make your letters more personal and about your donors?

Response Mechanisms: BRE and Donate Now!

Don't even consider sending any type of appeal without a response mechanism or way for donors to send in a donation.

BRE stands for Business Reply Envelope. It's the inner envelope that goes along with a mail appeal. At a minimum, it's self-addressed (back to the organization). It should also have pre-printed space for donors to write their contact information (including phone number and email address). BRE's do not need to be pre-stamped. Donors can put their own stamps on.

A donate now button should be prominently displayed on all electronic solicitations and your organization must be able to accept credit cards online.

Monthly Giving (Sustainer) Program

A monthly giving or monthly sustainer program is an automated program for donors who choose to give on a monthly basis. A sustainer program is a great way to significantly increase your annual fund donations. In order to implement a monthly giving program, the technology must be in place to charge a donor's credit card or deduct from the donor's bank account on a monthly basis.

The benefit of a monthly giving program is that it enables you to upgrade donors from one giving level to another. For example, if you have a $50 annual donor who is willing to give $10 per month instead, you have just upgraded them to $110 per year, more than doubling the annual donation. Yes, there are additional fees associated with operating such a program, but if done well, the benefits far outweigh the costs.

You might want to hold a special campaign to see how many of your annual fund donors you can convert to sustainer members, and increase their giving in the process. Challenge your board members to come up with a creative way to register fifty new donors to join the program in a

Schedule of Bulk Mail Solicitations			
	Traditional Mail	Electronic Mail	Notes
January		Recurring Donor Club	
February			
March	Spring Appeal	Spring Appeal	
April	Spring Newsletter w/ BRE		
May	Event Invitation	Event Invitation	
June	Bequest Mailing		To large and loyal donors only.
July			
August			
September	Fall Appeal	Fall Appeal	
October	Fall Newsletter w/ BRE		
November	Holiday Appeal	Holiday Appeal	
December		Clean-Up Appeal	To those who haven't donated yet this year.

specified period of time. Maybe they would be willing to issue a challenge match, where board members contribute a dollar for every dollar given by a new donor, up to a certain amount.

Budgeting

Make a budget for your direct-mail appeals. Remember to include the following costs:

◆ Printing (letters and brochures, etc.)

◆ Postage

◆ Mail house costs

Return on Investment—Measuring Results

Before you send a mail appeal or email solicitation, come up with a goal. Write down how much money you hope to raise, the number of responses you hope to get, the average gift size, number of repeat donors and more.

Be realistic when setting goals and expectations.

Schedule of Bulk Mail Solicitations

When embarking on your annual campaign, it's important to have a schedule of solicitations for the year planned out in advance. A sample calendar of bulk solicitations is on the prior page. Adjust yours to fit your organization's needs and budget.

To Recap

◆ Bulk mail is an important way to grow your base of support by acquiring new donors and increasing donations from existing supporters.

◆ A comprehensive bulk mail program must include traditional (snail) mail solicitations and electronic solicitations.

◆ Personalization is key to success with bulk mail.

◆ Bulk mail may cost more than it generates in the first year. It is a long-term fundraising strategy.

Chapter Seven

Face-to-Face Fundraising: Facing Your Fear

IN THIS CHAPTER

···→ Why face-to-face fundraising is so important for your organization.

···→ A specific plan of how to get started with personal fundraising.

···→ All the details you need on how to identify, cultivate, solicit, and steward donors.

···→ The difference between annual and capital campaigns.

A well-known statistic in the field of philanthropy is that more than 80 percent of philanthropic dollars come from individuals, and less than twenty percent of donations come from corporations and foundations combined. My guess is that your organization's revenue picture looks almost the opposite and you receive more than half of your fundraising revenue from corporations and foundations and less than half from individuals (not counting government funding). If this is the case, then this chapter is for you. It's time to get into the wild world of individual fundraising and significantly increase the amount of money your organization raises each year.

Although individual fundraising can be the most profitable and cost effective form of fundraising, many nonprofit organizations shy away from face-to-face fundraising, preferring instead to raise money through grant writing and special events.

Of course, many nonprofit executives and board members focus on grant writing and event planning because they appear to be the simpler types of fundraising. However, once you begin the process and have some early success, you will see how important fundraising from individuals is to the future of your program.

Fundraising is all about relationships. Your goal is to build a relationship between the organization and the donor (one that will outlast your time at the organization). The reason that "face-to-face" is so important is that you can't build relationships with donors if you don't meet with them.

Think about your relationships with friends and family. They take effort, although hopefully not too much effort. In order to maintain good relationships, you need to keep in touch, provide updates, maintain a level of trust, and get together periodically. It's the same with donor relationships!

Annual versus Capital

A capital campaign is a special, one-time fundraising effort that can span several years, for a specific project or expense—often a building or renovation project.

See Chapter Six for the definition of annual fund.

As I discussed in Chapter Six, your annual fund is the money you need to raise to operate your ongoing programs and services. Capital, on the other hand, refers to one-time special expenses. Using your house as an example, your annual expenses include groceries, electricity, water and gas bills. Capital expenses, on the other hand, are things such as needing a new roof or furnace.

For the current time, while you practice fundraising from individuals, focus on increasing your annual fund and don't worry about capital campaigns. It will be extremely difficult, if not impossible, to launch a capital campaign if you don't have a solid annual fund in place.

In Chapter Six I discussed the importance of bulk mail for the annual fund. Now, I will explore the role of face-to-face fundraising for your organization. Face-to-face fundraising can, and should, significantly increase your annual fund income. Here's how.

Identification

As you understand from Chapter Two, there are four stages to the fundraising cycle.

Identification is the first stage of the fundraising cycle, where individuals (or corporations or foundations) are identified as potential donors. Although it might seem obvious to identify potential donors, many nonprofit professionals and board members don't have any idea who their good prospects are or even who their current donors are.

I was recently facilitating a board meeting at a hospital foundation. We were discussing prospect identification, and a board member we'll call John said, "How about Donald Trump?" I responded, "Great idea! Do you know Donald Trump?" John was silent for a second and said, "no." I gently continued, do you know if Donald Trump has been a patient at this hospital? Again, the response was a more timid "no."

When I said, "great idea" in response to John mentioning Donald Trump, I certainly meant it. If a board member at one of the organizations I'm working with knows someone of great wealth, I definitely want to know about it. However, volunteers need to understand that fundraising is about relationships, and you can't raise money from someone just because they're "rich."

It certainly wasn't my intention to embarrass John, but I wanted to make the point that Donald Trump was, in fact, NOT a good prospect for this organization in spite of his well-known wealth.

stories from the real world

While it would be nice if we were all connected to Donald Trump and other super-wealthy individuals, the fact is that most of us aren't. Only approximately 1 percent of people are in the Donald Trump category, so we probably know lots and lots of people who aren't in this category.

The challenge for you and your board members is to identify people with the ability to give (regardless of the amount) and have an interest in the organization.

When beginning the identification process, you will want to identify two groups of people: first, your largest donors, and second, your most loyal donors. These two groups will make up your best prospective donor list, or group of "prospects."

Largest Donors

The first people to identify when trying to determine who you will solicit face-to-face are your largest current donors. One reason that it's important to have a database is because this is where you will find your best individual giving prospects.

Identification is the first stage of the fundraising cycle. It is where individuals, grant makers, corporations, or other potential donors are identified as such for your organization.

A **prospect** is an individual, foundation, or corporation that has been identified as a potential donor for your organization.

definition

When looking for your largest donors, run two reports from your database. The first will be a list of your largest donors. For example, everyone on your list who gave over $1,000 or $5,000 or $10,000 in the last two years.

The second list is a list of your largest donors with their giving totaled, or cumulative giving. Be sure to run this list in addition to the first list of large, one-time donations. This list will capture those donors who come to all of your events, purchase raffle tickets, and give an annual fund gift. Their total giving in a given year adds up to a large gift, but none of their individual gifts would have qualified them for the large-donors list.

Largest and Most Loyal Donors List

Donor Name	Giving History	Primary Contact	Cultivation Plan	Notes

Loyal Donors

To identify your loyal donors you need to run a separate list of people who have given five or more times. Loyal donors are those individuals who give year after year. Loyal donors are different from your largest donors. Their pattern of repeat giving makes them special and you will want to know who they are, regardless of the amount they gave.

You should now have three lists:

1. Largest single-time donors
2. Largest donors identified only by totaling their annual or lifetime giving
3. Loyal donors

If the lists are long (more than thirty donors each) then raise the criteria and run them again. For example, if you searched for people who gave over one-thousand dollars and fifty names came up, then up your search criteria to donor's who gave more than five-thousand dollars to come up with a lower number of names to work with.

Share the three lists with your board and staff members. Have a discussion about any individuals on the lists that they know. Find out how they know the individuals and what they know about them in terms of their giving ability and philanthropic nature.

Merge your lists into a "top twenty" prospects list, and include those individuals you will cultivate and solicit this year.

If you don't currently have a list of donors you will need to begin with "friend-raising." Friend-raising is a made-up

---

To identify donors to solicit face-to-face this year:

1. Generate list of your largest and most loyal donors.

2. Discuss prospects with board and staff members to help narrow lists.

3. Merge and purge the list to a number you can manage (between twenty and thirty).

to do

term in the world of philanthropy to refer to acquiring supporters for your database or list, before they are converted into donors.

Whenever I am working with board members and they need help figuring out who they know, I use a basic spider grid to help get their minds going. I then ask them to identify every group of individuals they know.

The same thing should be done with the organization in the center, as shown here.

Spider charts can help with friend-raising and the identification process. Use with board members as a visual tool and exercise to help identify prospective donors for your organization.

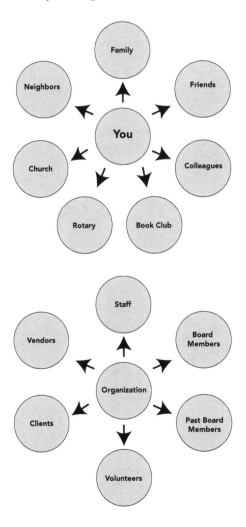

Cultivation means relationship building in the world of fundraising. It is a process whereby prospective donors and representatives of an organization (board and staff members) get to know one another. During cultivation, a prospective donor should learn more about the organization and the organization (board and staff members) should learn more about the potential donor.

finition

Cultivation

Cultivation is the second stage of the fundraising process and refers to relationship building. Relationships are so important to fundraising because successful fundraising is built on trust.

The reason why walk-a-thons are so popular and often fantastic fundraising events is that their success is based on participants (walkers) soliciting friends, family, and colleagues to support them. It's much more likely that someone will give if a friend (the walker) asks than if the organization were to ask directly. This is because the relationships are already established and if the walker believes in the organization, then the donors will too.

Similarly, the reason that social networking has such fundraising potential is that relationships and trust between "friends" and "followers" is already established.

There are many ways to build relationships. Think about how you build relationship with new friends. You meet them somewhere. You get a feeling of connection and/or discover that you have something in common. Then someone invites the other to a meal or out for coffee so you can learn more about one another. If both parties have a good time another date is made where you learn even more about each other.

Building relationships between an organization and a prospective donor is similar. Each party brings something to the relationship and the relationship develops over time with a series of "getting to know one another" meetings.

First Meeting: Talk Less, Listen More

The next step in individual, face-to-face fundraising is to take your list of top-twenty prospective donors and schedule meetings with each of them.

Scheduling a first meeting can sometimes be a challenge. I've heard every excuse there is to not meet. In some cases, certain individuals are truly not willing to meet with you, although they will continue to support your organization. However, if someone has been a strong supporter of your organization, then you want to do everything in your power to convince them to meet with you, even for only fifteen minutes. As I mentioned, it's hard to build strong relationships by phone and email. Meeting in-person is the number one way to connect with someone, so getting the first meeting is key. Everything after that is a piece of cake.

I suggest that you create a list of possible excuses that people might give you to not meet and have counter-arguments for each one (without getting argumentative, of course). Here are some examples to get you started:

◆ Them: I'm too busy. You: I understand your time is tight and I want to be respectful of it. I would be happy to meet with you at your home or office at your convenience for fifteen minutes, just to say thank you and provide you with a quick update.

◆ Them: I can't give more, so there's no reason to meet. You: I will not be asking you for money at this meeting. I'm really interested in meeting with you to learn more about why you have given in the past. I also want to thank you in person for all the generous support you have provided.

Don't worry if your efforts are unsuccessful. Keep the people who won't meet with you on a "B" list and send them invitations, program updates, invitations to take tours and volunteer, and more.

By moving people from your "A" list to your "B" list, it makes space on your "A" list for new names.

At the First Meeting

You might have heard the well known expression, "we were created with two ears and one mouth, because we are supposed to listen twice as much as we speak." Since most fundraisers are type-A and love to talk (myself included), speaking less can be significantly challenging for many of us.

Unfortunately, a mistake that novice fundraisers often make is thinking that it is their job to tell prospective donors as much as possible about the organization without stopping to take a breath.

When you are fortunate enough to schedule a meeting with a donor, make it as productive as possible. Here are some topics you are sure to want to cover in a first meeting:

Recently I worked with a group of executive directors from a statewide children's advocacy organization. One came up to me and said she hated asking. She felt that what I was talking about, in terms of relationship building, was "fake and phony" and not about genuine relationships.

I asked if both she and the potential donors cared about the well-being of the children, and, if so, suggested that a genuine relationship could be based on that. There's nothing fake about bonding over your mutual passion for a cause.

 **stories from the real world**

- ◆ Express gratitude for their prior giving

- ◆ Explain how their gift was used

- ◆ Provide an update about recent successes and setbacks

- ◆ Ask advice

- ◆ Invite them to become engaged (volunteer)

- ◆ See the list of open-ended questions (beginning on the next page) for additional topics of conversation

The rule of thumb is that you should only talk twenty percent of the time and listen eighty percent. Do this by asking smart, open-ended questions.

Cultivation Activities

In addition to an in-person meeting, there are many ways to cultivate prospective donors. The important issue is that each cultivation effort result in the individual learning more about the organization *and* someone from the organization learning more about the individual. Cultivation activities should also play an important role in the fundraising cycle and lead toward the next gift.

Examples of good cultivation activities include things like:

◆ Meetings in person (at the home or office of the individual or at the organization)

◆ Tours of the organization

◆ Volunteer activities

◆ Event attendance (fundraising or otherwise)

◆ Reception at the home of a board member

You might have noticed that I don't mention "lunch." That's because lunch can be complicated for a variety of reasons, which I will go into in greater detail in the next section on solicitation.

Open-Ended Questions

The goal of cultivation is to build relationships that will support and benefit the organization. You should ask open-ended questions in order to get to know a potential donor and make certain you are not doing all the talking. Here are examples of some good open-ended questions:

◆ Why are you interested in this organization?

◆ How did you get involved in the first place?

◆ Why did you decide to donate here and why do you continue to donate?

◆ What makes you decide to make donations to this organization, or any other?

◆ Would you like to get involved, and how? Present them with a list of possible volunteer opportunities.

◆ How is our organization perceived in the community?

◆ What do you like most about our organization?

◆ What changes would you like to see made to our organization, programs, services?

◆ Do you know other people who might want to learn more about our organization? Would you make an introduction?

◆ How would you like to continue your support of the organization? Present a list of organizational needs. Make it clear that you are not asking for a gift at this time, but want to have a conversation about what the organization needs and what the donor might be interested in supporting at a later date.

Goals and Outcomes

The goal of cultivation is to prepare you to ask. By the time you get to asking, it should not be a surprise to prospective donors. The cultivation process should prepare them to be solicited.

When I worked at a battered-women's shelter, we considered $5,000 a major gift, because we received less than ten $5,000 gifts per year. When we did, it was a major event! On the other hand, when I worked at Rutgers University, we didn't consider a gift in the "major" category unless it was $25,000 or more, while just down the road at Princeton University, major gifts started in the million dollar range. All major gifts, at very different levels.

On the same note, I worked for a homeless shelter where all board members were expected to give $1,000. This was a major gift for some board members and no big deal for others.

stories from the real world

Cultivation Plan Template

Getting to know a prospective donor takes time and effort. Before asking face-to-face for a gift, it is important to get to know the person well and have multiple contacts (or touches). Make a plan for your top prospects and include the following touches before scheduling a meeting to ask for a gift:

Volunteer Opportunities				
Additional Touches (Tour, Attend Event, etc.)				
Send Information or Update				
Follow-Up				
First Meeting				
Prospect Name				

Solicitation

The next stage of the fundraising cycle is solicitation or the actual ask. Although each stage of the fundraising cycle is critical, without an ask, you probably won't get any gifts.

For the purposes of this book, we will be concentrating on increasing your annual fund. If you are just getting started, it is unlikely that you are involved in a capital campaign or would be asking for major gifts. The place to begin asking for gifts in person is for your annual fund. After success in this area for a few years, if there is a need, your organization might want to consider embarking on a capital campaign and asking for major gifts.

The term "major gift" means something different for every person and every organization. For one person a "major" gift might be $1,000 and for someone else it might be $100,000 or more. The same is true for organizations.

What to Say (Sample Language)

The important part of asking for a gift is to ask for a specific amount and for a specific thing. For example:

Solicitation is the actual "ask," or request for money (also referred to as a donation, contribution, or gift). I will use the term to refer to any request for funds, including a grant application, event invitation, appeal letter, sponsorship request, or in-person ask.

Major gift can be defined in many ways. A major gift can be determined from the perspective of the organization or from that of the donor. A specific gift amount might be a considerable gift to one donor, but not much at all to another. Likewise, one organization might consider $1,000 a major gift and at another, major gifts begin at a million dollars.

finition

◆ "I hope you will join us in supporting the after-school program with a contribution in the range of $1,000."

◆ "I'm here to ask you to consider a donation of $2,500 to support a new computer for the classroom."

◆ "We hope you will support the animal shelter's general operations with a donation in the range of $5,000."

You might notice that in some of the examples above, I used the word "range," but didn't actually give a range, such as $500 to $1,000. Can you guess what will happen if you ask for a range and actually give a range of amounts? If you guessed that they'll give the lowest amount, you're right. By asking for a "range" and then giving a single number, it still gives them wiggle room and you're not asking for a yes or no, black and white number. If you ask for a gift in the range of $1,000 and they give $750, you'll both still be happy, because they did what you asked.

The reason it's important to ask for a specific amount is that if you don't, the donor won't know what you expect. If you are not specific, the donor might write a check for $100, thinking that that's what you asked, even if you were hoping for significantly more. Also, if you don't ask for a specific

Before going with a board member to solicit a donor, be sure to practice before the meeting. Make certain that everyone attending the meeting (except the donor) understands the goals of the meeting, exactly who will make the ask, and how much you are asking for. Each meeting attendee should have a specific role. For example, the board member will open the meeting by thanking the donor for meeting, for the donor's past giving, and loyal support. Next, the executive director will give a brief program update. Finally, whoever is assigned to ask will do the ask. In order for the meeting to go smoothly, rehearsal and planning are essential.

practical
tip

amount, the donor will agonize over how much to give, not knowing what you want.

Who

The person who should ask the prospective donor for a gift is the individual who knows the person best. For example, if the individual is friends with a board member, it's best if that board member does the asking. That being said, a board member is often unable or unwilling to do the ask, in which case it will be up to a staff person—generally the executive director or development staff member—to do the asking.

Hopefully the board member will at least attend the meeting to be supportive and nod along, even if not actually making the ask. For many volunteers, asking is just too uncomfortable. Please understand that whoever ultimately makes the ask should be well known to the person being asked and should have been involved in the cultivation process throughout.

Also, if the solicitor (asker) is a volunteer, this person needs to have already made a gift. This is important because it's much easier to ask someone for a donation if you can say "join me" and "I've done my part, I hope you'll help too."

What

As mentioned above, it's important that you ask for a specific item, program or service, even if what you're asking for is unrestricted operating money. People like to know what they are giving to and supporting. Be specific. As long as you've had discussions in advance about the importance of operating funds, and the prospective donor seems to understand and appreciate the importance of it, it's a perfectly acceptable thing to ask for.

When

There is never a perfect time to ask, so the right time is now.

You will probably never feel prepared enough. There will always be more research and cultivation you could do. However, if you want to raise more money for your organization, you will need to get to a point in the cultivation process when you are ready to ask. You should be ready when you have had at least one preliminary conversation with the person you are asking to support the organization and you feel that the person is committed to supporting the organization in some meaningful way.

Schedule a meeting time at the convenience of the prospective donor.

Where

It's important to make an ask wherever the person being asked feels most comfortable. That could be the person's home or office, or even at your organization. Avoid asking for a gift at a restaurant or other food establishment where it could be noisy or you could be interrupted.

How Much

One of the many questions I am asked frequently is how to determine how much to ask for. This is much more of an art than a science, and there's no exact number. The ask amount generally comes from a combination of factors, including:

◆ Giving history

◆ Interest and commitment to your organization on the part of the donor

◆ Financial situation

◆ Philanthropic nature

As I've mentioned, a person could be generous, or philanthropic, in nature, as well as have a deep commitment to and passion for your organization. However, if the person doesn't have the capacity, or financial resources, to make a gift, the gift can't be made. So, while ability is a major factor, it's only one factor, because those who have the resources might not have any interest in doing so.

That said, it is your job during the cultivation process to determine how much you will ask for. It will be important to have honest conversations with prospective donors about what they would be interested in supporting and at what levels. Before you go to an ask meeting, you should have decided on a specific dollar amount.

Stewardship

The way you thank your donors can have a major impact on future gifts. Therefore, it is important that you thank your donors sincerely and frequently. Some examples of ways to thank your donors include:

> Stewardship is the final stage of the fundraising cycle and is the process of thanking and following-up with a donor after a gift is received. The thank-you is an important part of the fundraising process and should be conveyed multiple times, in multiple ways.

- ◆ Letters

- ◆ Handwritten notes

- ◆ Email

- ◆ Phone

- ◆ In person

- ◆ Listing in publication (newsletter or annual report)

- ◆ Listing on donor wall

Thanking can also take place by multiple people. For example, the executive director can send hand-written notes while a board member makes thank you calls (or vice versa.)

To Recap

- ◆ Individual, face-to-face fundraising is one of the most important and underutilized methods of fundraising by small- and medium-sized nonprofits.

- ◆ Use individual fundraising to significantly increase your annual fund.

- ◆ Begin by making a list of potential donors, or identifying prospects.

◆ Cultivate donors by building strong relationships and learning about why they give to your organization.

◆ Solicitation is the asking part of the process, including who, what, when, where, why, and how much.

◆ Thank donors after receiving a gift to ensure repeat gifts in the future.

Chapter Eight

Simple Planned Gifts that Anyone Can Manage

IN THIS CHAPTER

···→ Why bequests are such an important component of a good fundraising program.

···→ How to get started asking for bequests.

···→ Who are your best bequest prospects and how to ask them.

···→ What to do with bequest money you've received.

Planned giving can be a foreign or scary concept for board and staff members who are unfamiliar with it. Most nonprofits are not engaged in the practice of raising planned gifts because of the myth that planned gifts are complicated or difficult. However, they can really be quite simple and produce extraordinary amounts of income for your organization.

One of the reasons why many people find fundraising so difficult is that talking about money is taboo in our culture. Put money together with death, and you really have a subject that makes people squirm. However, if you are able to re-frame the conversation and focus on the importance of leaving a legacy, the conversation magically takes a turn to something happy and desirable. This new conversation is about the opportunity to make the biggest charitable gift of a lifetime.

If you are successful at soliciting bequests, your organization will reap the rewards for many years. Just consider how much easier your life would be now if someone a decade ago had been soliciting bequests for your organization. If so, these gifts would be rolling in and benefitting you now!

Although it is unlikely that you will see the results of your efforts on planned giving, it is critical for the long term stability of your organization that you put some effort in that area. One of the best strategies I know for organizations to launch endowment funds is to solicit bequests.

After reading this chapter, you will know that planned gifts can be complicated or simple. You and your organization can solicit them without much effort on your part and they can generate huge amounts of money for your organization, now and in the future.

There's a saying in our field, that once a person adds a charitable bequest to their will, it automatically guarantees that the donor will live another ten years. That will always bring a smile to your donor's face.

Getting Started

The most important thing you need to know about planned giving is that approximately 90 percent of planned gifts in this country are bequests. That leaves only a small percentage of planned gifts that are complicated, including gifts of real estate, charitable remainder trusts, charitable lead trusts, gift annuities, and more.

To get started, all you need to do is focus on bequests. Don't worry about the others for now. If you do come across someone who wants to make a more complicated gift, consult a "partner professional" who can discuss the details with you.

> A **planned gift** is a charitable donation that requires planning on the part of the donor and has tax benefits. Donors should consult their own professionals when considering a planned gift, including their attorney, accountant, and financial planner to make certain that the gift is beneficial to them, in addition to the charity.

finition

Accepting bequests is generally fairly simple on the part of the charity, assuming that the wording and address are correct in the donor's will. Below is a sample of a real organization's bequest language:

The following four types of gifts direct a gift to the XYZ Organization.

Percentage:

"I give to the XYZ Organization, a nonprofit corporation of the State of [organization's state], located at [address], _____% of my estate."

Specific:

I give to the XYZ Organization, a nonprofit corporation of the State of [organization's state], located at [organization's address], (Choose one or more)

❑ The sum of $_____.

❑ _____ shares of stock in _____ Company.

❑ My real property commonly known as _____.

Ask your organization's attorney to review the language before publishing it or giving it to a potential donor. Nonprofits should not be providing any legal, tax, or financial advice to donors. Ensure that your donors consult with their own professional advisors.

important

Residual:

"I give my residual estate to the XYZ Organization, a nonprofit corporation of [organization's state], located at [organization's address]."

Contingent:

"In the event of the death of any of the beneficiaries, I give to the XYZ Organization, a nonprofit corporation of the State of [organization's state], located at [organization's address], _____ (percentage, specific, or residual language as above)."

Once you have the official language approved by your attorney, you're ready to solicit bequests. It really is that simple.

Create a Legacy Society

Once you have decided to actively solicit bequests, you might want to consider creating a legacy society. Legacy societies are used to cultivate and steward planned gift donors. Develop some basic rules about who can join and how to join. It can be as simple as anyone is included who notifies the organization about including a planned gift for the organization. Since bequests are revocable gifts, meaning they can be changed at any time while the donor is living and legally competent, there's no need for confirmation or proof. If donors are willing to share documentation of their planned gift, that's great too.

Revocable refers to planned gifts where donors can change their minds at any time. Because bequests are revocable planned gifts, it's important to continue to cultivate and steward these donors for the reminder of their lives.

Irrevocable is a term used for planned gifts where donors cannot change their minds, such as with charitable gift annuities and charitable remainder trusts where the donor does not reserve the right to change the charitable remainder interest.

(de)finition

Hold a reception, luncheon, or dinner in honor of legacy society members each year. Encourage them to share their plans with others as a way to spread the word. Talk about any planned gifts that have been realized and what it means for the organization. Acknowledge your members' generosity and treat them like VIP's.

Whom to Ask?

Identifying planned giving prospects is really quite simple. Remember that list of loyal donors I had you create back in Chapter Seven? That's your list of bequest prospects as well.

Your best prospects for bequests are individuals who have a strong connection to your organization and mission. They should be individuals who have been donating for a minimum of five years (usually longer) at any level. Yes, even people who have donated twenty-five dollars per year for more than ten years are great bequest prospects. People who leave charitable bequests are individuals who have been giving throughout their lifetime, which means ten or more years.

Once you think about it, it's obvious that people would only leave bequests to organizations that are a major part of their lives, either directly or indirectly. How likely are you to leave a bequest to an organization you were only involved with for a short while? After all, it's their legacy we're talking about.

Add charitable bequests to the list of things you will discuss with your best and most loyal prospects. Begin with current and former board members. Ask them to consider including your organization in their wills.

What About a Donor's Family?

People without children are your best planned giving prospects. Do not disregard this important piece of information. If you have loyal donors without children, you should target them first for including your charity in their will.

However, while it's true that many more people without children leave charitable bequests, people with families also leave money to charity in their wills. When speaking with people with children about leaving a bequest, it might be helpful to suggest that they think of their life and legacy as a pie. Ask them to consider what has been important to them during their lifetime and what they want to be remembered for.

The pie chart illustrates how you can have a conversation with a prospective bequest donor. You might say something like:

Since XYZ organization has been an important part of your life for many years, I hope you will consider leaving a bequest so our important work can continue into the future. If they have children add something like: I understand your family is important and of course it comes first. We would be delighted to be included at any level or percentage.

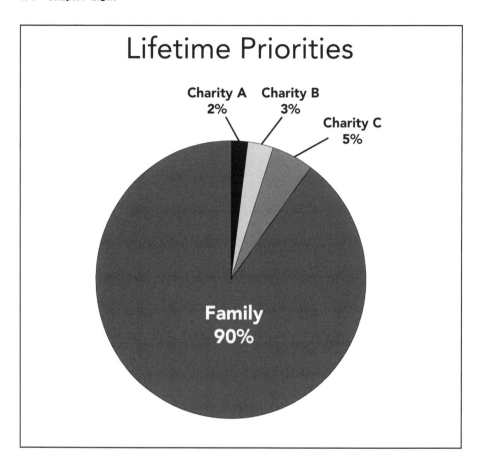

Lifetime Priorities

Charity A
2%

Charity B
3%

Charity C
5%

Family
90%

Bequest giving is often an opportunity for donors to make the most significant gift of their lifetimes and that will be important to some donors.

As an example for people with families, the *Lifetime Priorities* pie chart illustrates how an estate can be divided up to show that the family comes first.

Demonstrating something like this will show donors that they can care for their family while still remembering charities and organizations that have played an important role in their lives.

Advertising Bequests

Although there's no replacement for asking people to consider charitable bequests in person, it is also important to advertise the fact that you accept bequests in a variety of other ways. Demonstrate how easy it is to create a charitable bequest on your website, in your newsletters, and other marketing pieces. Some reasons it's important to do this are:

◆ You won't be able to ask all of your prospects in person and you want to be able to reach as many people as possible with your efforts.

◆ Sometimes donors will identify themselves to you as bequest prospects based on your marketing efforts and you don't want to miss those opportunities.

◆ Not all donors will be ready to include a bequest at the exact moment you ask. Your marketing efforts will serve as regular reminders, and hopefully, when they are ready to include your organization in their will or add a codicil (will attachment or amendment), your information will be readily available and in front of them, literally and figuratively.

As I was doing research for this book, I came across a website that listed the following reasons for making a testamentary gift:

◆ Simplicity

◆ Flexibility

◆ Tax relief

While these all are technically true, they are unlikely to motivate a donor to leave a bequest to your organization. It would be more meaningful to the donor to say something like:

Reasons to leave us in your will:

◆ Leave a legacy of your life

◆ Provide a clean environment for future generations

◆ Continue to help find a cure for cancer

Do you see a difference between the two sets of reasons to leave a bequest?

When people are drafting their wills, they are thinking about what's going to happen when they're gone. Get to the heart of the issues.

Allied Professionals

Allied professionals are accountants, lawyers, and financial advisors, who serve as resources for nonprofits and donors in the event of a more complex planned gift. You should encourage donors to use their own advisors. And, you can have your own list of trusted advisors to recommend at the request of a donor. They are also a great resource for you in the event that a donor comes to you with a more complicated gift idea.

> Do not ever put yourself in the position of giving or appearing to give legal or financial advice to any donor, in writing or verbally. Utilize professionals for all legal, tax, and financial advice.
>
>  practical tip

Asking for the Gift

The best way to receive bequests, just as with any donation, is to ask for them. It's not that people aren't interested in or willing to leave a bequest, but it's often that it hasn't occurred to them. Studies have shown that most people are willing to consider charitable bequests once asked.

What are you waiting for? Go out and ask.

Investing Your Bequests

In my opinion, funds received from bequests and other planned gifts should be used to create or grow an endowment fund. They are unique gifts and should be used to leave a legacy for the donor and long-term benefit of the organization, if possible. Income from bequests might be your only opportunity to start or grow an endowment fund, as they are one-time, often relatively large gifts. If you use bequest income for your annual fund, your annual income will be highly uneven and unreliable.

Just consider how wonderful it would be if your own legacy to your organization is that you helped establish an endowment fund that provides some relief to the annual operating budget. Although few small nonprofit organizations have endowments large enough to fund a significant portion of their budgets, having an interest-generating endowment is a wonderful help.

To Recap

An **endowment fund** is an investment fund established by a nonprofit, where the principal is not used, but a percentage of the interest generated by that fund is used for operations and programming. Donor-designated endowment funds are legally binding (the organization typically cannot touch the principal except in unusual circumstances).

- ◆ Bequests are the most frequently established type of planned gift.

- ◆ Bequests can make a huge difference in your fundraising efforts and ability to start or grow an endowment fund.

- ◆ Bequests are one of the easiest types of planned gift to ask for and accept. Anyone can do it, including you!

- ◆ Your best bequest prospects are your long-time loyal donors, without children.

- ◆ Start with bequest language provided in this chapter and have your organization's lawyer approve of the language you select before adding it to your website and printed materials.

Chapter Nine

Event Fundraising and Corporate Sponsorship

IN THIS CHAPTER

···→ The secret to event fundraising.

···→ The real role of event committees.

···→ Why sponsorships are key to fundraising success.

···→ How to develop event timelines and budgets.

If you're part of a new development office at an organization with no special events program, you have an amazing opportunity in front of you. You have a chance to create any type of event you like and recruit an amazing committee of volunteers to help you. Unfortunately, many new nonprofits create a series of small, only marginally profitable events. Instead, I recommend creating one signature event and going all out.

If, on the other hand, you're at an organization that already has several fundraising events, you should analyze them to determine which are worth doing and which need to stop. If your events are making money, raising friends for the organization, and spreading the word about your good work, then they are probably worth continuing. If your events are not making much money then you want eliminate them, which is not always an easy thing to do.

In most cases, new organizations err on the side of too many events. Start-up boards and founding executive directors see events as the primary way to raise funds and often begin by having one event after another. Unfortunately, events are actually the most expensive and labor intensive type of fundraising. Having too many events wears out staff and volunteers (and loyal donors) and often doesn't raise nearly as much money as they should for all the time and talent that goes into them.

My recommendation is that you choose one or two signature fundraising events that you will have this year and in the future. It's important to have an annual event for the following reasons:

◆ The event will get easier each year, because you will know what needs to be done and will have a template for execution.

◆ Attendees will include the event on their annual social calendar and come to enjoy attending your event each year.

◆ Sponsors often include your event in their budgets from year to year, thereby allowing for some continuity in sponsors.

◆ Holding new events each year causes you to start from scratch on fundraising and logistics.

I would always prefer an organization have one or two signature events, rather than lots of small events all year long.

Special Event Basics

Pros (reasons to have events)

◆ Raise unrestricted operating money

◆ Raise friends (grow mailing list)

◆ Spread mission

Cons (reasons to be cautious)

◆ Expensive

◆ Time consuming

Sadly, many organizations are having "fundraising" events that barely break even. Of course, if you don't raise money, it's not actually a fundraising event at all. Board and staff members justify having these under-producing events year after year as good cultivation events. There's nothing wrong with having cultivation events, as I will discuss later in this chapter, but don't have them by accident simply because your fundraising event didn't raise any money.

Special Event "Rules"

At your next special event:

- ◆ Be sure to mention your mission.

- ◆ Tell your story or provide a testimonial.

- ◆ Thank your sponsors and donors.

- ◆ Collect contact information of all attendees.

- ◆ Meet new friends and cultivate existing ones.

- ◆ Raise tons of unrestricted money—don't lose money.

- ◆ Follow up with attendees and cultivate further.

Ask yourself if you are following the above rules whenever you are making a major decision about your special event.

For example, have you ever had a special event where you didn't mention the cause? If so, you broke one of the rules. I've heard all the excuses such as, "the room isn't set up to have speakers," or "we don't

With my guidance, a mentoring organization changed how it planned its signature fundraising event. Instead of relying on staff to plan and raise money for the event, it formed a committee of volunteers (board and non-board members) to help with fundraising.

In one year, it doubled its income. By making one relatively minor, but important change, it was able to raise new and increased sponsorships with a small handful of new committee members who had access to corporate sponsorships.

stories from the real world

want to interrupt people's good time." These are not good excuses to miss an opportunity to share your case with a room full of your best prospects.

Events as a Cultivation Opportunity

In addition to raising money, fundraising events provide a wonderful opportunity to raise new friends for your organization and build relationships with existing donors and supporters. Events also enable

---

The number one secret to successful event fundraising, which is unknown to many board members and novice professional fundraisers, is that most fundraising events are made or broken on sponsorships. Ticket sales will never raise as much as an event with sponsors.

Let's say you're having a fundraising dinner and the cost of the dinner is $50 per person, which covers the venue, food, and gratuity. You decide to charge $100 per person and make $50 per head. However, you have not yet taken other costs into account such as invitations, entertainment, centerpieces, awards or plaques, audio/video, or any other costs.

Once all costs are accounted for, for the sake of this example, let's say you are still netting $25 per person. If 100 people buy tickets, you've only raised $2,500, which is not a lot of money for the amount of work you've done.

If you're raising sponsorships for the same event, and you get four sponsors (one at $1,000 and three at $500 each) you've raised the same amount of money from your first four donors (sponsors) as you did from selling 100 tickets.

You might believe that obtaining sponsorships is more difficult than selling tickets, but it's not. Once you have the right committee in place, attracting sponsors is as easy, if not easier, than selling tickets.

example

---

you to spread your message, tell your story, gain new donors, build buzz around your organization, and have a great time.

Your organization might also choose to have some cultivation events that are not fundraisers. These events are important and worthwhile too and should be included in your annual expense budget. One example of a non-fundraising cultivation event is when you invite donors and prospective donors to attend a lecture or event for free where they will have a good time and learn about your organization.

Forming a Committee

The best way to raise lots of money at your special events is to have a well-connected and dedicated fundraising committee.

Whenever I speak to a group about fundraising events, I ask the following question: "Do you have an event committee that is responsible for selecting the venue, menu, entertainment, centerpieces, and give-a-ways?" I refer to these types of committees as "fund-spending" committees, as opposed to fundraising. They work very hard and end up spending lots of money on the event, and not ever raising much money. You don't need a committee full of people to plan logistics. Event planning can be handled by staff, plus one or two key volunteers, if necessary.

All other volunteers should be utilized for a true fundraising committee, where committee members bring in sponsorships and sell tickets and tables. Other committee member roles can include:

◆ Deciding on the type of event to have, if it's a "first annual."

◆ Identifying and recruiting honorees and keynote speakers.

◆ Determining appropriate sponsorship levels. (More on that later.)

Develop a committee member job description and start recruiting volunteers for your new event committee today.

Sponsorship

As I mentioned above, sponsorship is the key to successful event fundraising. Your ability to raise big sponsorships will depend, in part, on the committee members you have around your table. You will want to set your sponsorship levels according to the type of event you are having and the committee members you have helping you.

For example, you might not be able to solicit a $10,000 sponsorship for a small community spaghetti dinner. On the other hand, $10,000 is an easily attainable sponsorship level for a benefit gala dinner in New York City.

Sponsorship is sometimes a business transaction, so keep the sponsor's needs in mind. The sponsor is expecting return on its investment in the form of increased sales, visibility, etc. In exchange for sponsorship dollars, you can provide whatever will give the sponsor high visibility, but won't cost you money. This can include things such as its logo on your website, on the invitation, in your newsletter, and listing on all event related materials and signs. These sponsorship benefits are low cost (to you) and high visibility (for the company).

You will want to base your sponsorship levels on the ability of the individuals on your committee to generate sponsorships. For example, if you have the CEO of a major corporation on your committee, you might have access to a $25,000 sponsorship through their corporation. On the other hand, if your committee is made up of local small business people, they might only be able to access sponsorships in the $500 to $1,000 range.

You want to make sure that the sponsorship levels you create are appropriate for those on your committee, so that committee members can be successful in soliciting sponsors.

In general, I recommend having about three sponsorship levels (fewer than three is too few choices and more than five is too many). The top level should be so high that if you get one, you jump for joy, but if you don't, it's no big deal. It should give you something to reach for and serve as a motivation to think big!

Your mid-level sponsorship should be an amount that several of your committee members feel they might have access to. You should be able to get one or more middle-level sponsorships. Finally, you want lots of sponsors at your bottom level; at least five.

If you are fortunate enough to get more than a handful of the top-level sponsors, then your levels are probably too low. On the other hand, if you can't get any sponsors at your top two levels, then you've set your sponsorship levels too high.

Sample Sponsorship Form

XYZ Organization and Logo
Awards Dinner

Date_____

Time _____

Location _____

Honorees and Speakers _____

Sponsorship

❑ GOLD SPONSOR $10,000
- ✓ Table of Ten (10 Tickets)
- ✓ Premium Full Page Ad in Program (front inside, or back inside or outside)
- ✓ Name/Logo on Signs at Event
- ✓ Logo/Link on website for 1 year
- ✓ Name on Invitation (if committed by print deadline – 00/00/0000)

❑ SILVER SPONSOR $5,000
- ✓ One Table of Ten (10 Tickets)
- ✓ Full Page Ad in Program
- ✓ Name/Logo on Signs at Event
- ✓ Logo/Link on website for 1 year

❑ BRONZE SPONSOR $2,500
- ✓ One Table of Ten (10 Tickets)
- ✓ Half Page Ad in Program
- ✓ Name/Logo on Signs at Event

❑ TABLE SPONSOR $1,500
- ✓ One Table of Ten (10 Tickets)
- ✓ Half Page Ad in Program

Tickets

❑ Individual Ticket ___ @ $XXX
❑ Member Ticket ___ @ $XXX

Name _____

Company Name _____

Address _____

Phone _____

Email_____

Checks payable to XYZ Org

Name (as it appears on card)

_____

Credit Card Number

_____

Expiration Date

_____

Security Code

_____

Signature

_____

Total $ _____

I cannot attend, but would like to make a donation of $ _____

Return to XYZ Org at address

Questions? Please call xxx-xxxx

List Event Sponsors

List Dinner Committee or Board Members

Each fundraising committee member should be willing and able to solicit one or more sponsorships for your special event.

One important point to keep in mind is that most of your sponsors should be solicited well in advance of the invitations being printed. First of all, you want your sponsors' logos to be printed prominently on the invitation. And second, it is unlikely that you will get sponsors as a result of your invitation. Sponsorships are generated through personal contact with committee members.

Logistics and Timeline

In order to have a well-planned and successful fundraising event, you will want to create a timeline and task list. Planning should start almost one year before your special event, especially if you're planning this event for the first time.

The first thing to do is to recruit an event fundraising committee. Once the committee is recruited and some primary decisions are made, such as what type of event you will have, you will need to pick a date and a location. Next comes recruiting honorees and speakers. Still well in advance of your event (eight months or so) you will want to start soliciting sponsors.

Many states require a gaming license for games of chance, such as raffles.

important

If you are having an auction or raffle, factor those in as well. Find out if your state requires a gaming license for your raffle.

The following is a sample timeline and task list. When creating your own, start with the day of the event and work your way backward. Feel free to use this sample as a guide.

Depending on the size and scope of your event and of your organization, the people who are responsible for the various tasks might be different. In general, a staff member such as a development director or special events person would be the primary person responsible for the logistics and coordination of a special event. If your organization doesn't have development staff members, or has a very small development office, you may rely more heavily on volunteers for event planning.

Event Timeline

Date	Task	Responsible Party	Notes
12 Months Out	◆ Recruit committee ◆ Determine event type ◆ Select date ◆ Book venue ◆ Create a budget		
6 -10 Months	◆ Identify honorees ◆ Identify speakers ◆ Recruit key sponsors ◆ Secure vendors (A/V)		
6 Months Out	◆ Recruit sponsors ◆ Plan agenda for event		
4 Months Out	◆ Order invitations		
3 Months Out	◆ Review menu and agenda with facility		
2 Months Out	◆ Mail invitations ◆ Order plaques		
1 Month Out	◆ Sell tickets		
2 Weeks Out	◆ Call donors to confirm attendance ◆ Print program/ journal		
1 Week Out	◆ Create nametags ◆ Make seating chart ◆ Meet with staff about roles and responsibilities		
Day of the Event	◆ Arrive at venue as early as allowed to ensure set up.		

Finances and Budgets

You will want to create a revenue and expense budget when considering your special event.

After creating a basic budget, you will understand how much you need to raise and how much you can afford to spend. Monitor these budgets closely throughout the process to make sure you're on track.

In order to raise the funds budgeted, plan on identifying two to four prospective sponsors for each sponsorship you need, as well as four to five times as many ticket buyers for the tickets you hope to sell.

Sample Expense Budget

Item	Projected Cost	Actual Cost	Total
Venue/ Food	$50 per head @ 200 people		$10,000
Invitations Print/ Design Postage/ Mailing			$3,000
Microphone/ Podium/ Sound			$400
Plaques/ Awards	$25 each times 4		$100
Program Booklet	$4 each @250		$1,000
Decorations/Centerpieces	Donated		
Giveaways	Donated (or none)		
TOTAL			$14,500

Sample Revenue Budget

Revenue Type	Amount	Quantity	Total
Gold Sponsorship	$5,000	1	$5,000
Silver Sponsorship	$2,500	2	$5,000
Friend Sponsorship	$1,000	5	$5,000
Tickets	$100	100	10,000
TOTAL			$25,000

The Day of Your Event

Assign staff and volunteers to different jobs. Have someone extremely competent at the registration table who is specifically in charge of walk-ins and table mix-ups.

Event day is often stressful, even for the most seasoned event planner. And, things will go wrong. The question is, how will you react when they do?

Whatever's happening, keep your head and keep your cool. There are always volunteers and donors within earshot and yelling never solves anything. If you feel like you're starting to lose your cool, step outside and take a breather. Be polite and do the best you can.

Assign board members to meet and greet guests at your special event and serve as ambassadors for your organization. Don't seat board members together, but spread them out around the room. Place one board member at each table, if practical, so they can answer questions and help generate conversation. Give them each talking points and suggestions in advance.

practical tip

Be sure to debrief after the event, so you can identify successes and learn from your mistakes for next year.

Professional Event Planners

Depending on the type of event you are planning, internal staffing, and your needs, you might want to consider hiring a professional event planner. Each individual event planner has strengths and weakness, so be sure to get referrals and check references. They also provide a wide range of services, some of which you will want more than others. For example, some are simply there to help with logistics, while others will help with fundraising too. Be certain to find out if they will help with fundraising, and if so, how. Of course, hiring outside help will add a significant expense to your event, but might be worth it.

Making the Most of Your Special Event: Follow-up

One of the key fundraising techniques associated with a special event is the opportunity to cultivate prospective donors and follow up with them soon after your event. If you skip this important step, you are missing an important opportunity to connect with prospective donors and new friends for your organization. Hopefully attendees will be euphoric after your special event and feeling great about your organization. This is the best time to get a meeting with them. If you wait too long, their enthusiasm will have dissipated.

Most development staff members are so relieved and tired after their event is over that they barely have the energy to send out thank-you letters, much less start making follow-up calls and scheduling appointments. If you want to ride the enthusiasm coat tails of your event, however, you will want to take advantage of this unique moment when people have you on their minds in a significant and meaningful way.

Be prepared for the post-event follow-up before your event takes place. Know the top ten people with whom you would like to follow up, assuming they show up for your event. Be sure to connect (speak) with them at the event and let them know that you would be interested in meeting with them individually, in a more intimate setting. If they seem receptive, ask them if you can call them next week to schedule something.

Once you've made the connection, follow up! Don't let a week turn into weeks before calling. When you have the green light for a meeting, refer back to Chapter Seven about working with individuals.

To Recap

- ◆ There are pros and cons to special events, so invest your time and resources wisely when planning them.

- ◆ Don't have more than two or three major fundraising events per year or you will wear out your volunteers and staff.

- ◆ Eliminate some of your smaller events that are not generating very much revenue, and put additional efforts into your more successful events.

- ◆ Recruit a fundraising committee for the event to help solicit sponsorships and sell tickets.

Chapter Ten

Grant Writing and Foundation Funding

IN THIS CHAPTER

- ···→ How to research and identify grant funders for your organization.

- ···→ The best ways to build relationships with funders, and why relationships are important.

- ···→ How to complete your grant application and determine the right ask amount.

Grant funding is a great way for many organizations to obtain seed money and get their start. Many foundation funders love to provide funding for new and innovative ideas and programs. On the other hand, many funders will only fund organizations with track records of success and a proven ability to spend donations responsibly. Regardless of where your organization is on that spectrum, you are likely an attractive candidate to at least a few foundations. The question is, how to find them and show them that you are worth funding?

It is also important to remember that donations from foundations and corporations comprise only a small fraction of the philanthropic dollars donated each year (individuals give the bulk of the money) so you should not spend all your time and effort chasing grants.

Grant writing is just like any other type of fundraising, meaning that it is about relationship building. Sending in "cold" applications is often unsuccessful and frustrating. If you build a relationship with foundation funders, and "warm" the funder up to your cause and your nonprofit, you are much more likely to be successful.

Sometimes even the best-written applications get rejected for no apparent reasons while less well-written applications receive funding. It is often because the foundation officers or staff members are familiar with the good work of the second organization and can overlook a poorly-written application because of a relationship history with the organization.

Types of grants—Government, Foundation, Corporate

There are several types of grants available, including government, foundation, and corporate. Each type has pros and cons and might or might not be right for your organization. To get you familiar with them, below is a brief description of each.

Government

There are three types of government funding—federal, state and local. Government grants can be a wonderful source of funding for many organizations, although funds for government grants seem to be declining each year. These grants are often large and generally come with an enormous amount of restrictions and requirements and are highly competitive.

Unless you are already familiar with a government grant that is appropriate for your organization, you might want to consider skipping this potential source of income for now. I generally advise new and smaller organizations to avoid government grants due to their high level of competitiveness and lengthy reporting requirements. Many small nonprofits do not have the infrastructure to meet government reporting requirements.

Foundation

Foundation grants are the most widespread type of grant, which most nonprofits receive at one point or another. These are privately funded foundations and can be very large or extremely small. Some family foundations only give out a few thousand dollars per year to their favorite charities, while large foundations give away millions annually. Private foundation application and reporting requirements range from complex to simple. Some foundations accept unsolicited applications and others don't. Small family foundations without staff members often only give to pre-selected charities because they don't have the resources to screen applicants. Larger foundations generally have formal guidelines to follow when applying for grants. Be sure to follow these directions and meet deadlines to increase your chances of receiving funding.

Corporate

Corporate foundations are similar to private foundations, and almost always have specific guidelines and formal application requirements. Corporate foundations are linked to corporations and often have limited scope in terms of what they will fund, which is often tied to business objectives. For example, pharmaceutical companies generally give to healthcare-related agencies and issues. Companies give grants for a variety of reasons, but they often want to raise their visibility in the community. On your website, in your newsletter, and at your events you must be sure to promote those companies that support you.

Research and Identification

As with all other types of fundraising, you cannot apply for grants until you have completed step one of the fundraising cycle—identify the grants you will apply for. It is important to research which grants are available and appropriate for your organization.

My personal favorite database for researching grants is the Foundation Center, which can be accessed for free at many locations (at the Foundation Center's offices located in NYC, DC, Atlanta, Cleveland, and San Francisco) as well as in many public and university libraries throughout the country. It can also be accessed for a fee from your desktop (via the Internet).

When researching grants, you want to look for a few factors that will indicate a good match and a high potential for funding. These factors include geography, mission, and type of funding.

Geography

Most funders have geographic restrictions about where they provide grants. They might be limited to specific cities, counties or states. Others will limit by country (either the US or others throughout the world). Be sure to first screen potential funders by this important, yet basic, criterion. There's no reason to apply to a foundation that only gives funding in California if you are in New York.

Mission or Scope

The next thing you'll want to look for is to what types of causes or organizations the foundation gives. It's important to find a funder with a good mission match to your organization. Many foundations give to a wide variety of causes, but you will want to make sure that you are a good fit, otherwise it's unlikely that you will receive funding. For example, if you are an organization that serves children, make sure the funders you apply to fund children's programs. To take it a step further, if you are a preschool, there's no sense in applying to funders that only support higher education, even though both list "children" and "education" as part of their criteria. Read guidelines carefully to make sure your organization is a good match with the potential funder.

Find out what organizations, programs and projects the foundation has funded in the past to see if your organization is a likely candidate for funding. This information (past grants) is often posted on the foundation's website or listed in its annual report. If you cannot find this information, try calling the foundation to ask if it has a list of past awards available. This information will also help you determine how much to request.

Types of Funding or Support

Each funder will provide specific types of support and you will want to make sure your needs also match these criteria. Most funders give program support. Others give to capital expenses or unrestricted operating expenses. Be sure that the funders you apply to give the type of money you are seeking.

Completing Your Research

After researching grant makers in a database, continue your research by going to the websites of the grantors you want to apply to. In other words, don't stop research based on what you find in databases. If you plan to apply for funding, go to each funder's website to get current guidelines and other information. If a funder doesn't have a website, call to ask for application guidelines.

After completing your online research, you will want to ask your staff and board members if they know anyone at the foundations you have identified (or at any others). Relationships are key to receiving grant funding, which will be covered in the next section. If you have a pre-established relationship (a member of your board knows someone at a foundation) then your chances of receiving a grant increase exponentially.

Take time to complete the following Grant Research Worksheet, which will give you a complete picture of your research results. If your research yielded great results, you might have more grant opportunities than you can handle and will need to narrow them down.

Only apply to those funders that give the largest grants *and* who are most likely to fund your organization.

Building Relationships

Building successful relationships is key to successful grant writing, just as in every other type of fundraising. For some reason, this seems counterintuitive to many fundraisers who feel they can send in "cold" applications.

Remember, the individuals making grant decisions are people too. Unless it is actually a blind grant review process, where the name of the organization has been eliminated from the application and reviewers literally don't know whose application they are scoring, then personal bias will be a factor. And, blind review processes generally only occur with government grant making, and won't be a factor at most foundations or corporations.

Grant Research Worksheet

Funder Name	Website/ Contact Info	Application Deadline	Possible Ask Amount	*Compatibility Ranking	**Decision to Apply

* Compatibility Ranking: Indicates how close of a match your organization is to the foundation. In part, this will help determine whether or not you ultimately decide to apply to that funder.

** Decision to Apply: You will not necessarily decide to apply to every funder you find. For example, a foundation might have a complicated application process, rigorous reporting standards, and only give $1,000 per grant. This application is probably not worth your time. Place a "yes" or "no" in this column.

When you build relationships with foundation trustees and staff, your chances of receiving funding increase exponentially (if they like you and your organization). This is because your organization has an advocate inside the boardroom.

Although it is important to have a well-written application, there are clearly times when even well-written applications are overlooked because no one in the room has ever heard of the organization applying. Similarly, poorly written applications are sometimes funded

> Rank those funders you have identified as "A," "B," or "C" by how likely they are to fund your organization. Include your ranking in the "Compatibility Ranking" column of your Grant Research Worksheet.
>
>  practical tip

by foundations with a history of working with the applicant or due to a good reputation in the community. Ideally, you want to have a well-written application and a relationship with the foundation to ensure the best chances of receiving the grant.

So what are some ways to build relationships with potential funders?

Networking

The first step in trying to build a relationship with a potential funder is to find out if an existing relationship already exists. Ask your board and staff members if they know any of the staff or board members at the identified foundation or corporation. If yes, then use that connection to start building a formal relationship between the two organizations. If no, dig a little deeper. Use social networks such as Facebook and LinkedIn to ask your networks if they know anyone at the foundation you are applying to.

Phone Call

If you can't identify an existing connection or relationship, you're going to have to start from scratch. The best way I know to build a relationship is to talk to someone, so pick up the phone. Before you do, do your homework. Be sure to have reviewed the foundation's website, guidelines, and any other information you can find. When calling a foundation for the first time, have some questions prepared to ask.

Start the conversation by telling the person that you would like to apply for a grant and have some questions. Examples of some questions you might ask include things such as:

◆ Are you making grants to new organizations this year?

◆ I've researched your grant giving range online and see that you give a wide range of funding. We would like to apply for $10,000. What would you recommend for a first-time applicant?

◆ There are two programs we are considering applying for. Would it be possible for us to discuss them for a minute and you let me know which sounds like a better fit?

◆ Do you have any words of wisdom for new applicants?

◆ Are you interested in coming to visit our program?

Invite

Build relationships with foundation funders by inviting them to see your program in action. They may not come, but they will know that if they want to come, they are more than welcome. Invite them to fundraising events, on tours, and to program events.

Mail

Add current and potential funders to your mailing list (traditional and email). Send them your newsletters, annual reports, invitations, and other items that you might be mailing.

Maintain Relationships

Once you have taken the time to initiate a relationship, be sure to maintain it. Communicate regularly with funders to provide program updates, major achievements, and setbacks. Yes, funders do want to know about setbacks. This is especially important if you are not going to achieve what they funded you for.

Grant Writing

Grant writing can seem intimidating and daunting at first, but is also the method that many organizations utilize to get their start-up and program funding. Don't be intimidated. Take the necessary steps to write good grant proposals.

> People give to people. This truth applies to grant funders as well as individuals.
>
> **observation**

- ◆ You are already taking the first step by reading this book.

- ◆ Buy a grant-writing book.

- ◆ Take a free class on grant writing at the Foundation Center or other nonprofit center in your area.

- ◆ Write a grant and ask an experienced grant writer to proofread your work. Be open to suggestions and criticism.

- ◆ When you are able, hire an internal staff member or external consultant to help you with grant writing.

Learn as much as you can before writing your grant. Ask good questions and be sure you have the most up-to-date guidelines.

Remember to state prominently the amount you are asking for. A big mistake organizations occasionally make is to submit a request, but neglect to say how much they are asking for. The reason for and amount you are requesting should be in the cover letter or somewhere on the first page of your application (unless it is asked for in another area).

Letter of Intent

Some funders request a Letter of Intent (LOI) before accepting a full application. A LOI will help a foundation determine whether they want to review a full application. A LOI should be less than three pages and on your letterhead. You should clearly state how much you are requesting and what the funds will be used for. Finally, you should provide a brief history of the organization, as well as a program summary.

Grant Funder Cultivation Worksheet

This worksheet will help you create a basic cultivation plan for grant funders. Be sure to "touch" each funder multiple times every year with updates and invitations. Feel free to use this sheet, or create your own. In addition to new potential funders, I recommend including existing grant funders, as they need cultivation too.

Place a date in each column when you plan to accomplish each cultivation activity.

Funder name	Initial phone call	Invitation to take a tour	Thank you note/call after grant is received	Call or email with program/ grant update	Invitation to event (fundraising or otherwise)

Application Sections

Each funder will have different requirements, but here are some sections that are common.

- ◆ Cover letter or executive summary

- ◆ Organization history

- ◆ Mission statement

- ◆ Program summary

- ◆ Request amount

Attachments

Each funder will request the specific attachments it requires. Below are some commonly requested attachments. Keep documents easily accessible in electronic and paper format for use with grant applications.

- ◆ Program budget and/or organizational budget

- ◆ 501(c)(3) tax determination letter

- ◆ List of board members with affiliations

- ◆ Bylaws

Make sure to attach all requested materials before submitting your application.

Follow Guidelines

Carefully review the guidelines provided by foundations. Highlight, circle or underline any key pieces of information, such as deadlines, page limits and font size, attachments, and any other requirements they have.

You don't want your application tossed in the reject pile simply because you neglected to pay attention to the details. If you are asked for one original and one copy, do that. If it specifies how the application should be bound (staples, paperclips, etc.), do it. Sometimes it comes down to the smallest detail.

Ask persons from outside your organization to read your grant application to make sure they understand what you are asking for. They should check to make sure you haven't used any industry jargon without explaining it and that the application makes sense to someone outside the field.

practical tip

Proofreading

Answer each question carefully. Let me say that again. Be sure to answer each question as asked. If something needs clarification or if you're unsure what the application is asking for, call the foundation.

There's nothing that screams "unprofessional" more than typos, grammatical errors, spelling mistakes and other errors. Once you've completed several grants, you will get into the habit of cutting and pasting materials from other grants. Be sure to do so carefully.

Once you've proof-read your grant proposal, give it to someone outside of your organization to make sure you haven't used any jargon and that they understand what you are asking for.

Determining how much to request.

There are several ways to determine how much to request. The key factors in deciding how much to ask for are:

◆ What is the range of grants the funder provides?

◆ How much do you need?

Clearly, you shouldn't ask an organization for $100,000 if its top grant amount is $10,000. That would be ridiculous. However, if a funder gives a wide range of grants, then ask for whatever you need, provided your request is well within its range.

Also, funders do not usually like to be the lone funder of any program or project. Make sure they understand that they will be sharing the cost with other funders.

Online Applications

Many foundations and corporations are transitioning to online applications. Most, if not all, online applications allow you to enter and exit your application as often as necessary prior to the deadline. When you encounter an online application, go into the application and identify the questions you will need to answer. Write your answers offline and cut and paste them into the online application.

Grants Calendar

List all of the grant applications (new and renewal) you will complete this year.

Funder Name	Contact Information	Application Deadline	Report Deadline(s)	Request Amount	Amount Received

Total Requested: $_____

Total Received: $ _____

To Recap

♦ Be sure to research sources of grant funding carefully to identify those you will apply to each year.

♦ Build relationships with current and prospective grant funders to ensure your best chance to receive grant funding.

♦ Meet all funder deadlines. Follow guidelines exactly. Include all appropriate attachments.

A Final Word From the Author

Next Steps and Parting Thoughts

I want to leave you with one final thought: fundraising can be fun and easy! Anyone can fundraise, including you and your board members. In this book, I have provided you with fundraising fundamentals and a template for success which, if applied, will significantly boost the amount you raise for your organization.

Whether you are brand new to philanthropy or have been in the field of fundraising for many years, I hope after reading this book you understand the fundamentals of fundraising or have reinforced many of the best practices that you already knew. You should be feeling optimistic, energized and enthusiastic about fundraising and the future of your program. Attitude is half the battle in fundraising! Your attitude determines whether you are discouraged and stuck behind your desk, or excited and out meeting with donors. This will make all the difference between success and failure.

It is my expectation that you now have the tools and confidence to run a professional fundraising program. If you came to this book a novice, understanding fundraising only from your experience with college dance-a-thons, high school team car washes, and PTO bake sales, you should now understand fundraising in a whole new way.

Most importantly, get out there and ask for contributions for your organization. The biggest mistake that fundraisers can make is getting bogged down in paperwork and office politics, and therefore never leaving their desks to meet with donors. I wrote *50 A$ks in 50 Weeks* to help individuals like you identify prospective donors for your organization and create a plan to get out and ask them. Remember, if you don't ask, you won't get.

I truly hope you'll use the concepts and worksheets in this book to jump-start and propel your development efforts to a whole new level. Keep it on your desk and use it as a reference. If you do apply the concepts every day, I promise you'll raise oodles more money than you would otherwise. Raising more money will bring you that much closer to achieving your mission, which is the overall goal.

Please let me know how this book has been helpful to you. I see this as just the beginning of our relationship. When you are able to apply some of the concepts and tools and raise more money for your organization, I want to hear about it!

Stewardship

Recently I was facilitating a board meeting, and one of the board members in attendance had just come from the dentist. He said he wasn't sure which part of his morning would be worse—going to the dentist or talking about fundraising. I promised him we would put the fun back in fundraising, and I think we did.

In the course of a few hours, I believe I changed his mind and his attitude. As a result, he will be a better fundraiser and advocate for his organization.

I hope after reading this book, you will be a better fundraiser and advocate for the cause and organization *you* are passionate about.

stories from the real world

Stewardship is such an important, yet often overlooked, part of the fundraising process. If I told you I had a secret weapon that would automatically increase your donor retention rates and move people up the donor pyramid, you'd want to know what it is, right? Simple—it's the "thank you!"

Donors should be thanked in multiple ways by multiple people. For example, this could mean having the executive director send handwritten notes, while a board member makes a call, and the development director sends an email. Sounds like a lot? How about for your top donors?

After all the work you've done to get new donors, the worst thing you could do would be to lose them. It's much more expensive to acquire a new donor than to keep an old one. So, keep the ones you've got by saying thank you!

Right now I would like to THANK YOU for all you're doing to make the world a better place. When fundraising has got you down, just think of all the people you are helping and remember that you are helping to make the world a better place.

Best wishes for all your fundraising success!

Index

If you enjoyed this book, you'll want to pick up the other books in the CharityChannel Press In the Trenches™ series, shown on the following pages.

And introducing Fundraising for the GENIUS, which kicks off our new GENIUS series published by our imprint For the GENIUS Press.

FUNDRAI$ING
as a Career:

What, Are You Crazy?

Linda Lysakowski, ACFRE

www.charitychannel.com

CharityChannel
PRESS

IN THE *Trenches*™

50 A$KS
in 50 Weeks

A Guide to Better Fundraising for Your Small Development Shop

Amy M. Eisenstein, CFRE

A Fundraising Planning Guide for:
- Development Professionals
- Nonprofit Executive Directors and CEOs
- Anyone else who wants to boost fundraising results

www.charitychannel.com

*Charity*Channel
PRESS™

In the Trenches™

Trenches™

ASKING™

about Asking

Mastering the Art of Conversational Fundraising™

M. Kent Stroman, CFRE

Discover how to:

- Equip staff and volunteers to raise *real* money
- Engage donors in the gift solicitation process
- Climb the *10 Step Staircase* and get your proposals approved
- Become more comfortable, confident and effective when asking

www.charitychannel.com

CharityChannel
PRESS™

YOU AND YOUR
Nonprofit

Practical Advice and Tips from the
CharityChannel Professional Community

This is surely the book I wish I had decades ago.
—Bob Carter, Chair-elect, Association of
Fundraising Professionals (AFP)

Edited by:

Norman Olshansky
Linda Lysakowski, ACFRE

www.charitychannel.com

PRESS

Trenches™

Capital Campaigns

Everything You NEED to Know

Linda Lysakowski, ACFRE

Discover how to:

- Conduct your capital campaign from start to finish
- Build a strong infrastructure for your campaign
- Develop a compelling campaign case statement
- Recruit volunteers for your campaign

www.charitychannel.com

*Charity*Channel
PRESS™

Confessions

of a Successful

Grants Writer

A Complete Guide to Discovering
and Obtaining Funding

Joanne Oppelt, MHA, GPC

A Guide for:

- Grant Writers
- Development Professionals
- Foundation, Corporate and Government Relationship Professionals
- Anyone Wanting to Raise More Revenue through Proposals

www.charitychannel.com

*Charity*Channel
PRESS

Trenches™

Getting Started in

Prospect Research

What you need to know to find who you need to find

Meredith Hancks, MBA

For those who want to:

- Jump-start as a prospect researcher
- Create an optimal research tool kit
- Build vital relationships
- Use data to guide fundraising strategy

www.charitychannel.com

*Charity*Channel

PRESS™

Raise More Money

from Your
Business Community

A Practical Guide to Tapping into
Corporate Charitable Giving

Linda Lysakowski, ACFRE

Raise more money for your nonprofit organization by:

- Identifying the types of businesses likely to give
- Communicating with business leaders in a more compelling manner
- Involving volunteers from the business world in your fundraising activities

www.charitychannel.com

CharityChannel
P R E S S

Fundraising

for the GENIUS™

The only book you'll ever need
to raise more money for your
nonprofit organization.

FOR THE GENIUS IN ALL OF US™

Linda Lysakowski, ACFRE

www.ForTheGENIUS.com

PRESS

Made in the USA
Middletown, DE
08 October 2014